JAPANESE CORPORATE FINANCE AND INTERNATIONAL COMPETITION

STUDIES IN THE MODERN JAPANESE ECONOMY

General Editors: Malcolm Falkus, University of New England, Armidale, New South Wales, Australia; and Kojiro Niino, Kobe University, Japan

An understanding of the modern Japanese economy remains both important and elusive. Its importance needs little stressing. From the 1950s Japan's economy grew at a rate unparalleled elsewhere and, despite recent setbacks, the economy remains strong and dynamic with increasing investment overseas. Indeed, Japanese-owned companies now produce more overseas than they do at home. Yet an understanding of this economic performance is made difficult by the wide cultural divide between Japanese and Western societies. On the one hand an understanding of the many unique features of Japan's economic and social life is essential if we are to appreciate the Japanese achievement but on the other hand this very uniqueness makes communication difficult. Straightforward translations of Japanese works frequently mean little to Western readers because the underlying attitudes and assumptions are so unfamiliar.

This series has been planned in the belief that there is a need for scholarly studies on the modern Japanese economy which are written by experts (both Japanese and Western) and aimed at Western readers. Accordingly, we have planned a series of books which will explore all the major areas of Japanese economic life. The books will present up-to-date material, and, where necessary, they will place Japan in its wider international context.

Japanese Corporate Finance and International Competition

Japanese Capitalism versus American Capitalism

Masasuke Ide
Executive Fellow
Nomura Research Institute
Nomura School of Advanced Management
Tokyo

First published in Great Britain 1998 by
MACMILLAN PRESS LTD
Houndmills, Basingstoke, Hampshire RG21 6XS and London
Companies and representatives throughout the world

A catalogue record for this book is available from the British Library.

ISBN 0-333-69597-6

First published in the United States of America 1998 by
ST. MARTIN'S PRESS, INC.,
Scholarly and Reference Division,
175 Fifth Avenue, New York, N.Y. 10010

ISBN 0-312-21158-9

Library of Congress Cataloging-in-Publication Data
Ide, Masasuke, 1942–
Japanese corporate finance and international competition :
Japanese capitalism versus American capitalism / Masasuke Ide.
p. cm. — (Studies in the modern Japanese economy)
Includes bibliographical references (p.) and index.
ISBN 0-312-21158-9 (cloth)
1. Corporations—Japan—Finance. 2. Competition, International.
3. Finance—Japan. 4. Capital market—Japan. 5. Japan—Economic
policy—1945–1989. I. Title. II. Series.
HG4245.I238 1997
658.15'0952—dc21 97-34873
CIP

This book is printed on paper suitable for recycling and made from fully managed and sustained forest sources.

10 9 8 7 6 5 4 3 2
07 06 05 04 03 02 01 00 99 98

Printed and bound in Great Britain by
Antony Rowe Ltd, Chippenham, Wiltshire

Contents

List of Figures ix
List of Tables x
Acknowledgements xii

PART I THE CENTRAL MARKETPLACE OF CAPITALISM

1 Economic Systems and Resource Allocation 3

1.1 The Three Types of Economic System 3
1.2 The Socialist Centrally Planned Economic System (Former Soviet Union) 8
1.3 The Pure Open Market Economic System (US Capitalism) 10
1.4 The United States as the Central Marketplace 12

2 Economic Value Creation by Investor-Owned Companies 17

2.1 The Economy and the Firm 17
2.2 The Process of Economic Value Creation through the Marketplace 18
2.3 Rules for Evaluating Company Performance 23

3 The Role of the Capital Market 27

3.1 Cash Flow as the Source of Value 27
3.2 Evaluation of a Company as a Going Concern 30
3.3 Diversification of the Source of Capital through 'Slicing' the Total Cash Flow 34

4 The Stock Market as the Final Judge of the Value-Creation Process **39**

4.1 Two Approaches to Stock Valuation: Technical vs Fundamental Analysis 39
4.2 Modern Portfolio Theory 41
4.3 Conditions for Efficient Stock Price Formation 44

PART II JAPANESE CAPITALISM

5 Japanese Economic and Financial Systems **55**

5.1 Strategic Allocation of Resources 55
5.2 The Indirect Financing System 60
5.3 The Financial Policy of Large Japanese Companies 63

6 The Unique Features of the Japanese Stock and Share Ownership Structure **69**

6.1 The Unique Share Ownership Structure 69
6.2 The Characteristics of Relationship Investment 73
6.3 Bank Asset Liability Management and Relationship Investment 76
6.4 High Valuation of Low-Profitability, Low-Growth Companies 78
6.5 Unique Features of Common Stock in Japan 81
6.6 Changing Patterns of New Equity Issues 82

7 Stock Valuation in Japan: Phase One **87**

7.1 Commitment to a Stable, Fixed Dividend 87
7.2 The Logic of Stock Valuation during Phase One 90

8 Stock Valuation in Japan: Phase Two **97**

8.1 The Proliferation of New Equity Financing at Market Price 97
8.2 Stock Valuation during Phase Two 103

9 Factors Underpinning the Call-Optimisation of the Stock Market **107**

9.1 The Downside Risk Hedging System 107
9.2 The Nature of the 'Japanese Beauty Contest' 108
9.3 Reconciliation of the Call-Optionised Market with Finance Theory 116
9.4 The Role of Main Banks as the Delegated Monitors of the Stock Market 117
9.5 Summary 120

PART III CORPORATE PROFITABILITY AND THE COST OF CAPITAL

10 Corporate Profitability and International Competition **125**

10.1 The Corporate Financing System as the Core of the 'Better and Cheaper' Strategy 125
10.2 International Comparison of Corporate Profitability 128
10.3 Low Profitability as an International Competitive Edge 133
10.4 Corporate Profitability and Corporate Growth 137

11 International Comparison of the Cost of Capital **141**

11.1 The Cost-of-Capital Concept 141
11.2 Empirical Findings 142

PART IV CRITICAL REASSESSMENT OF JAPANESE CAPITALISM AS A CATCH-UP MODEL

12 Japan's National Value-Creation Process 151

12.1 The Role of Companies 151
12.2 Japan's Economic Value-Creation Process 154

13 The Merits and Demerits of Japanese Capitalism 159

13.1 Japan's Excellent Macro Performance 159
13.2 Limitations and Weaknesses 164

14 The Future: New Challenges and Changes 173

14.1 New Challenges 173
14.2 Some Evidence of Change 180
14.3 Implications for the Strategies of Japanese Companies 183

Notes and References 187
Index 191

List of Figures

2.1	Value creation process by companies in the open market	19
3.1	Value creation and valuation: a five-year project	28
3.2	Value creation and valuation: going concern	31–2
3.3	Slicing the total operating cash flow	35
5.1	Comparison of the flow of funds to the non-financial sector	67
7.1	US–Japan comparison of the distribution of dividends per share	89
7.2	Typical stock price pattern	93
8.1	Long-term stock price trend of selected issues	100
8.2	Stock price changes	105
9.1	Trend of recurring profits	109
9.2	Cumulative value of ranking portfolio	115
11.1	International comparison of cost of capital	144
11.2	Cost of banks' equity capital	147
12.1	Japan's traditional value-creation process	157
13.1	Macroeconomic performance of selected nations	161
13.2	Volatility of real GNP	162
13.3	Growth of the automobile industry	163
14.1	Strategic options for value creation	183
14.2	New paradigm of Japanese management	185

List of Tables

1.1.	Economic systems as resource allocation mechanisms	5–7
5.1	Characteristics of the traditional financial system	58
5.2	The number of major financial institutions	60
5.3	Equity to total capital ratio of large Japanese and US companies	63
5.4	Trends in the profitability of large Japanese and US companies	64–5
6.1	Comparison of the stock ownership structure in Japan and the United States	70
6.2	Comparison of the nature of major shareholders	74
6.3	International comparison of corporate profitability and PER	79
6.4	Estimated expected return for investors	80
6.5	Changing pattern of new equity issues	83–4
6.6	Shift in the average stock price	86
8.1	Amount of relationship equity investment by the major city banks	101
9.1	Regression analysis in relation to fundamental variables and realised total return in Japan	111
9.2	Simulation results on recurring profits	114
10.1	Major market indicators	129–30
10.2	Financial performance of the Japanese and US company sector	132

10.3	Minimum required profitability of large Japanese and US industrial companies	134
10.4	Profitability of foreign direct investment	136
10.5	Profitability and PER of selected pairs of Japanese and US companies	138
11.1	International comparison of cost of capital	146
12.1	Management objectives and constraints contrasted	152
13.1	Japan's performance	165
13.2	International comparison of annual work hours	169
13.3	International comparison of labour productivity	170

Acknowledgements

The author and publishers wish to thank the following for permission to reproduce copyright material: Nomura Research Institute for Figure 9.1 and Table 8.1; Japan Security Analysts Association for Figures 11.1, 13.2, and Tables 9.1 and 9.2; Toshi Radar Inc. for Figure 8.1; Yamaichi Research Institute for Table 6.5, and Professor Burton Malkiel of Princeton for Table 11.1. Every effort has been made to contact all the copyright-holders, but if any have been inadvertently omitted the publishers will be pleased to make the necessary arrangement at the earliest opportunity.

Part I

The Central Marketplace of Capitalism

1 Economic Systems and Resource Allocation

1.1 THE THREE TYPES OF ECONOMIC SYSTEM

The modern economic system can be broadly divided into three types according to differences in the method of resource allocation. At one extreme is the socialist centrally planned system, as represented by the former Soviet Union. Under this system a relatively small elite group with a very large degree of power plans all resource allocation and implemention. At the other extreme is the pure open market system, such as that of the United States, where the process of resource allocation is left to the free market mechanism (the so-called invisible hand), in which all citizens participate.

However most nations adopt a mixed economic system, which combines the free market mechanism with state control of certain areas of resource allocation, taking a middle road between the two extremes. The economic and financial system that Japan has built up since the Second World War can be regarded as one of the most successful mixed economic systems. Together the American-type open system and the mixed systems form the capitalist market economy. Since the Second World War the United States has, in a manner of speaking, acted as the central marketplace of the world system, as will be explained in the pages that follow.

With regard to resource allocation, all economic systems ultimately have the same objective, that is, to make the best or most effective use of limited or scarce economic resources and to meet the people's various needs in the most effective manner. However, just as there are several routes to the top of Mount Fuji, there are many different ways of attaining resource allocation objectives. In fact the process of consensus building when setting priorities, the allocation mechanisms, the methods of performance evaluation and the reward–punishment rules can vary greatly between systems and it is very difficult to decide *ex ante* whether one is better than the others. Any system is a result of the nation's choice of the best allocation system to attain its priority objectives, reached by consensus under given resource constraints.

Accordingly, only time can prove the superiority or inferiority of an economic system. For example, since the fall of the Berlin Wall in 1989 it has became clear that the capitalist market economy is superior to the socialist centrally planned economy. The socialist regime that had for the past three quarters of a century rivalled the capitalistic regime and divided the world's political and economic system into two, reached a deadlock and admitted defeat. As a result the former Soviet Union and the Eastern Bloc countries have rushed headlong towards the establishment of a free market system.

With the overwhelming victory of the capitalist market economy it is natural that the issue of competition and the coexistence of different types of market-based economic systems are attracting serious attention. The Western nations no longer have to assume a unified ideological standpoint. Needless to say the Japan–US Structural Impediment Initiative (SII) talks and the highlighting of the differences between the Japanese system and that of the West came about against the background of such changes.

In the following pages I will provide an overview of the characteristics of the two extreme types of resource allocation, that is, the socialist centrally planned economic system and the pure open market system, as the framework for understanding the unique quality of the Japanese postwar economic and financial system. Table 1.1 compares the major characteristics of the different types of economic system and resource allocation mechanisms, as represented by the United States, the former Soviet Union and Japan.

TABLE 1.1 Economic systems and resource allocation mechanisms

		Market-oriented economic system	
	Centrally planned	Mixed or managed market economy	Pure market economy
Representative nation	Former USSR	Japan	USA
Primary mechanism for resource allocation	Planning, allocation and price fixing by central government	Free market mechanisms and strategic allocation by central authorities	Free market mechanism (invisible hand)
Primary entities for economic value creation	Central government and government-run-companies	Government-run companies and private companies	Private (investor-owned) companies
Competition among producers	No competition	Limited or regulated competition	Free competition under fair rules
Primary objectives of a company	National goals, public interest	Public interest, employment and profit	Profit (maximising return on capital)
Investment decision making	Central government (Communist Party, politicians and bureaucrats)	Government and private sector leaders	Business managers
Allocation of capital	Centrally allocated through government budget	Government, bankers, corporations and investors	Investors, bankers and managers of financial institutions

TABLE 1.1 *(Continued)*

		Market-oriented economic system	
	Centrally planned	Mixed or managed market economy	Pure market economy
Criteria of capital allocation	National priorities	National priorities and financial return	Financial return
Measures to control risk	Eliminating risk through planning and allocation	Planning and consensus – building, government intervention, protection and guaranty, building long-term relationship, grouping and Keiretsu, information sharing	Diversification and differentiation, protection of IPR, creating an efficient market, disclosure, professionalism
Investment vs financing decisions	Investment decision first, financing follows	Investment decision first, financing follows	Simultaneously through market
Money and capital market	Non-existent	Primarily a face-to-face market	Well-developed open market
Role of the government	Priority setting, all resource allocation and implementation	Priority setting, consensus building, industrial policy, guiding and coordinating, direct and indirect interventions in the market	Regulatory rules setting, overseeing, developing infrastructure, indirect intervention

TABLE 1.1 *(Continued)*

		Market-oriented economic system	
	Centrally planned	Mixed or managed market economy	Pure market economy
Necessary infrastructure	Big and powerful government, huge bureaucracy	Fairly big government and bureaucracy, formal and informal network of consensus building and control, long-term relations among government, bureaucrats and business sector	Small government and explicit set of rules of competition: fair trade laws, disclosure rules, accounting rules etc.; Large number of professionals such as lawyers, accountants, securities analysts, bond rating agencies, etc.
Primary method of responding to small changes in environment	Changes in the central plan	Industrial policy, persuasion and guiding through competition in the marketplace	Through marketplace, through free competition
Primary means of responding to major changes	*Coup d'état*, revolution	No established rules	Through election, or referendum
Primary objective of the economic system	Economic equality of the people	GNP growth and full employment	Maximizing the utilities of the citizens as a whole

1.2 THE SOCIALIST CENTRALLY PLANNED ECONOMIC SYSTEM (FORMER SOVIET UNION)

There are many variations of the socialist centrally planned system. However they all rely on the wisdom of a small group of elite to predict the needs of the nation and plan resource allocation without incurring the waste and risk that are inherent in the market economy, which allocates resources through trial and error and involves numerous participants in the market.

The production and supply of all goods and services are decided at the central government level according to priorities set by the leaders, and the national budget is allocated accordingly. Thus all economic activities are carried out by government-owned companies according to the central plans.

The major premise of such a system is that the elite who decide the resource allocation can accurately predict all the needs of the people. Should a gap arise between these needs and the plan, the plan has to be adjusted. The socialist economy does not have any established mechanism to match the surplus and shortage of economic resources among people.

Under this system all categories of goods, their quality, volume and price, and the allocation of all finished goods, intermediate goods and raw materials have to be decided and managed by someone. Unless somebody at the centre decides such matters as the colour and patterns of, for example, for the ladies' dresses, production will never commence. On the whole the public is unable to initiate value-creation activities according to their own judgment. It goes without saying that implementing and managing a system like this requires an enormous amount of bureaucratic and state power.

A problem with this system is that the value and the price of goods and services can drift far apart. The prices of goods and services are not determined by demand and supply in the marketplace, but according to political or social criteria decided unilaterally by the state. The most useful market-economy determinant of resources allocation, namely market price, cannot be used under this system.

Moreover this system does not allow individual citizens the freedom to pursue businesses opportunities that will better fulfill the needs of the people and make more effective or efficient use of limited resources. There is no incentive for the people to develop and implement better ideas, technologies, products and services, and no changes, improvements or up-grading can take place unless directed by the centre. The overwhelming majority of the people have no choice but to accept whatever is imposed on them by the government.

Such a system might have been workable and even desirable under the miserable conditions suffered in Russia during the last years of imperial rule, when the Soviet revolution broke out. The needs of the Russian people at that time were not only basic but quite clear, and it might have been possible for the ruling elite to know of these needs and to devise an economic plan to meet them. However, once this had been accomplished it proved impossible to fulfill the people's diverse further needs by planning alone. The biggest defect of the system was that there was no mechanism with which to adjust smoothly and flexibly to a more demanding environment once they succeed. Changes to the plan, which was the only possible way of coping with changes in needs, was strongly resisted politically, since that would have meant criticism of the planners themselves. This defect opened the possibility of political rebellion, riots, *coup d état* or revolutions.

The justification put forward for this system was that it would provide equality of income and wealth for all. However as all individuals are unique and differ in their characteristics, talents and tastes, it was not easy to bring about such equality. On the contrary, the socialist countries invariably featured a privileged class comprising party leaders and top bureaucrats, and few would believe that equality was being pursued in such a way as to satisfy the majority of the people. Thus we can say that the socialist centrally planned economic system was bound to collapse sooner or later.

1.3 THE PURE OPEN MARKET ECONOMIC SYSTEM (AMERICAN CAPITALISM)

Most nations now manage their economy through the market in some way or other, although the degree to which the market mechanism is used varies from nation to nation. In fact there are a great many variations of the market-based economy, and what is at issue today is how the different systems should compete and coexist. Successfully introducing a pure open market economy, in which virtually all resource allocation is left to the market mechanism and a large number of economic constituents freely participate, is easier said than done, and it requires a very strong belief in the system. The United States has adopted this form.

The United States represents an extreme type of market-based economic system in that it regards the market mechanism as absolute. For the present at least, the US system is regarded as the most universal version of the capitalist market economy. The United States is the biggest economic unit in the world, and the most basic characteristic of the US economic system is a strong belief in 'openness': the more participants there are in the market, the better the market will be and all participants will benefit. For this reason the US-type capitalist system imposes no restrictions on participation and it is regarded as most important to allow free entry at any time. Because of this the US system, despite being extreme, has become a valuable international public good.

However it is easy to come up with contradictions, such as Waiver Clause, which limits agricultural imports into the United States, and 'Buy American' legislation. If we are to prove empirically that a certain economic system is open, we can only do it by comparing it with other types of system. The Nomura Research Institute has measured five industrialised countries, including Japan and the United States, against an 'openness' index for (1) freeness, (2) fairness and (3) market openness. The United States came out on top for openness with 55.6, followed by Germany (50.6), Britain (50.4) and France (47.0), with Japan (46.4) at the bottom.[1]

In order to separate the pure open market from the mixed or 'managed' market economy system, especially that of Japan, I will call the former US capitalism from now on.

Under US capitalism, the activities that create economic value are performed by individuals or investor-owned companies. Production activities are mainly carried out by large corporations (joint-stock companies), but any individuals wishing to start their own business are free to do so at any time. As already mentioned, under the socialist centrally planned economic system, such freedom did not exist.

Under US capitalism, companies are no more than a means of performing economic activities in an efficient manner, and they can be dissolved or disposed of whenever the shareholders agree that there is no longer a need for their existence.

In practice, under US capitalism it is possible to buy and sell anything in the market – not only raw materials, machinery and equipment, labour, goods and services, but also technology, ideas, know-how, personnel, brand names, market shares and even entire companies. In the market, the prices set for all these resources reflect their fundamental economic value, as described in the following pages. And as long as they are willing to accept the market prices, anyone can participate in the market at any time and conduct unlimited transactions.

According to US capitalism, it is the obligation of the government to the citizens that the nation should develop and maintain such markets as to enable the citizens to buy and sell any commodity at an appropriate price whenever they need to do so. For this reason, the primary role of the government is to develop a framework within which to maintain fair market and fair competitive conditions and to ensure that the rules are adhered to. Because of this, nations modelled on US capitalism are sometimes called regulatory states,[2] and to manage such a system a large number of professionals such as attorneys, accountants, security analysts and credit-rating agencies are required.

The pure open market economic system is based on the neoclassical economic belief that if consumers maximise their utilities, investors their returns and companies their profits, this will result in the most desirable allocationof resources for the system as a whole. This system welcomes and encourages the participation of anyone who finds it in their interest, and emphasises the equal opportunity to participate, whereas the socialist and many other systems tend to emphasise the equal sharing of the economic 'results'. The major strength of the US system is that it continually adjusts itself to ever-changing economic realities through the market mechanism. And it can be said that the ultimate objective of the system is to maximise benefits and utilities for the citizens, who are the ultimate beneficiaries of the system.

1.4 THE UNITED STATES AS THE CENTRAL MARKETPLACE

It is important to understand why the Unites States has chosen such an extreme economic approach. At least at the outset, it can be considered that the reason has to do more with the uniqueness of the United States as a nation rather than its desire to act as an 'international public good'.

Firstly, it is a relatively new nation and consists of immigrants or their decendants from all over the world, especially Western Europe. It is a nation that has developed with openness in terms of flows of people, ideas, products, technology, and capital as the primary source of strength.

Secondly, being geographically large and richly endowed with land and natural resources, and with a large inflow of European capital from the early years of its development, the United States was ideal for the open market model in which a large number of participants employ various economic and managerial resources to trade or invest for profit.

Finally, many of the people who went to the United States in the early days were seeking freedom from pressure and oppression, such as that imposed by the Catholic Church or ruling monarchs. For that reason, ever since the founding of the nation various systems have been developed to respect and protect the basic rights of individual citizens, and to ensure the right to private ownership without undue oppression or exploitation by the government or any other major power. That is to say – based on lessons from history that too great a concentration of power, be it political or economic, often runs counter to the interests of individual citizens and consumers – much effort has been made to prevent the concentration of power. In the political system this has resulted in the separation of the three main powers, namely legislative, executive and judicial. In business system the power to allocate resources is spread among stockholders, boards of directors and managers, and very strict antitrust legislation has also helped to prevent the excessive concentration of economic power.

These antitrust laws have served to enable otherwise fragmented and weak consumers and small businesses to compete with large businesses by allowing them to enter in the market at any time. It is assumed that by so doing the system will keep attracting better products, services, technology, ideas and human talents to the market. As will be explained later in more detail, this should lead to the numerous needs of the citizens being met as efficiently as possible, as competition should result in better products at lower prices.

In addition to its own unique needs, explained above, as the champion of the allied nations the United States exercised powerful leadership in the reconstruction of war-torn Europe and Japan, and in promoting the economic development of developing nations since the Second World War. The United States has not only opened its vast domestic market, but has also offered other nations many kinds of economic and management resources, including ideas and know-how, technology, capital and human talents, and it has acted as the central marketplace or clearing house of these resources. Also, in order to further the development of an open, multilateral, international marketplace, the United States has championed the free trade system under the Bretton Woods regime.

It could be said that as a result of its openness, the US economic system is a type of international public good, serving the global community as well as the United States itself. Within the international economic system the US economy could be likened to a central marketplace for, say, the buying and selling of agricultural goods. Although this marketplace only accounts for a fraction of total transactions in agricultural products, it can be regarded as an important public good because surpluses and shortages of many agricultural products are adjusted at the least possible cost.

Thus the United States has come to act as the central marketplace of the entire capitalist market system, coordinating and adjusting surpluses and shortages of raw materials, manufactured goods, services, ideas, know-how, technology, human resources, capital and other economic and managerial resources for all nations and individuals that wish to make use of such a marketplace. In running this 'clearing house' the United States has provided a very valuable public service to all the nations and subsystems that constitute the market-based economic system. As long as the central marketplace exists, all nations, companies or individuals will be able to adjust the shortages or surpluses in economic and management resources by buying or selling them at the prevailing market prices.

The central marketplace has also enabled all nations to overcome resource limitations and geographical constraints, and to achieve economic and industrial growth. For example in the postwar period Japan, which is poorly endowed with natural resources and geographically small, was able to grow into a major economic and financial power largely because of the existence of the international market system. The vital importance of this to Japan's prosperity is illustrated by the fact that during the Second World War – when Japan was contained by the ABCD line (the America – Britain – China – Dutch blockade that cut off the supply of resources to Japan), which effectively closed the door to imported raw materials as well as preventing exports from Japan – the Japanese economy quickly ground to a halt.

To date Japan has been a mere participant in the central marketplace. However, in view of its economic prosperity and the degree to which Japan depends on the international market for its further development, it would be in the country's best interests to contribute actively to the further enlargement and development of the market. To this end it is vital for Japan to gain a proper understanding of the rules by which the market operates, and of the necessary conditions for the market to remain open to Japan. One of the main themes of this book is to clarify this point.

2 Economic Value Creation by Investor-Owned Companies

2.1 THE ECONOMY AND THE FIRM

In most capitalist market economies the creation of economic value is mainly performed by large investor-owned companies. However the relationship between the government and companies varies from one nation to another. Even in well-developed economies there are cases where the economic objectives of the nation and the activities of individual companies are not related in any direct way, as exemplified by the United States. Conversely there are cases where the two are closely aligned, as exemplified by Japan. Accordingly, within the capitalist market economy there can be great differences as to the management objectives of companies, industrial structures, financial systems, the relative importance of corporate profitability, employment and trade practices, the incentive and reward systems for managers and employees, and the way their performance is measured and evaluated.

As the central marketplace the United States has made an extreme choice in the relationship between the government and companies. In the United States it is assumed that commercial and economic activities should be left to the private sector, with minimal government involvement and intervention. Hence the US government tends to have a confrontational and regulatory rather than a friendly relations hip with business, in contrast with Japan, where government–business relations are friendly and close.[1]

This means that it is very important for us to understand the logic of the management of companies, the primary micro units of resource allocation and creators of economic value, in order to understand the logic of US capitalism as well as the function of the central marketplace. Therefore in this chapter and in Chapter 3 I will investigate the value-creation process by investor-owned companies under US capitalism, and how their performance is evaluated in the capital market.

2.2 THE PROCESS OF ECONOMIC VALUE CREATION THROUGH THE MARKETPLACE

Figure 2.1 illustrates an investor-owned company in an abstract and simple form comprising debt capital (*D*) and risk capital or stockholders' equity capital (*E*). The diagram shows how economic value is created by a company and how it is evaluated in the capital market.

Firstly, as shown in the centre of Figure 2.1, the value-creation cycle starts with the company going to the marketplace to purchase necessary resources (process 1). It then adds value to them (process 2), takes its products back to the market (process 3) and recovers the invested capital (process 4). The capital market will mainly evaluate the performance of the company according to how much it has added to the capital entrusted to it by investors at the beginning of the process.

In this system, one of the important rules of the game is that the market will wholeheartedly welcome individuals or companies that provide better and/or cheaper products than those currently available, as they will contribute to an increase in the utility of the entire market. The problem here is that if the market is well developed and sufficiently competitive, an average or mediocre attempt to create value will receive little praise and reward. Therefore almost all companies will try to add a unique value by differentiating their products or services from those of their competitors. This is shown by process 2 in Figure 2.1.

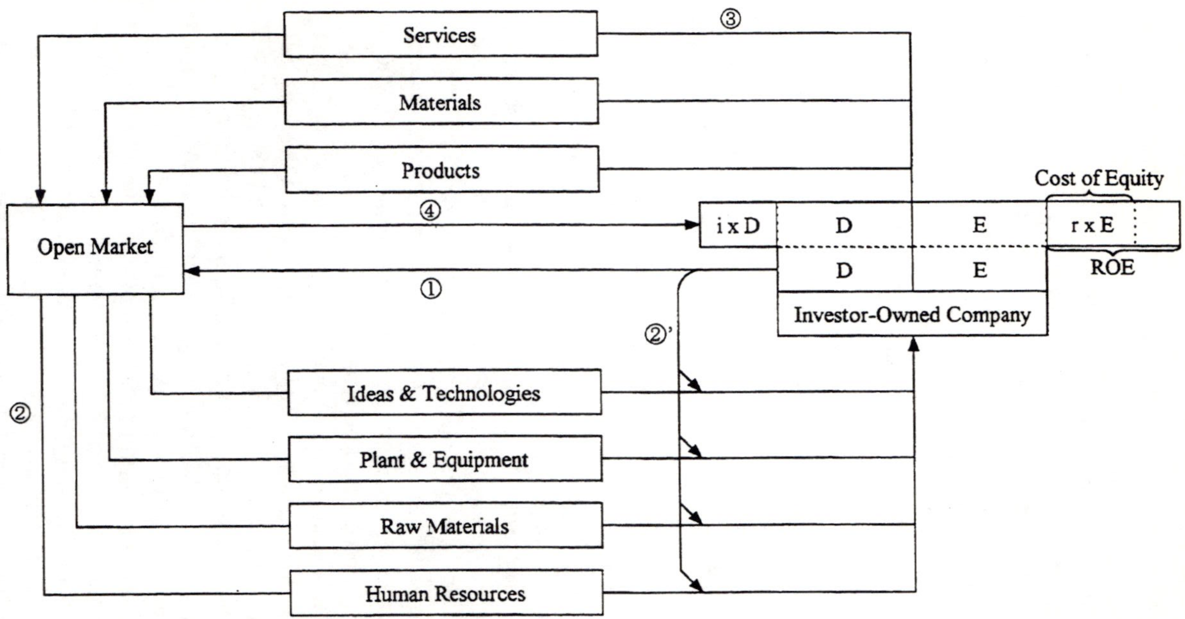

Notes: D = debt capital; E = equity capital; i = required return on debt capital (interest); r = required return on equity capital; see text for explanation of numbers.

FIGURE 2.1 Value-creation process by companies in the open market

This differentiation can be in the form of a new technological breakthrough, the development of new materials or unique production systems, or nurturing a corporate culture that promotes innovation and creativity. Through such activities companies try to develop unique values that can not be easily imitated by their competitors. Thus companies compete head to head to provide better and/or cheaper products than those currently available.

The concept of 'better and/or cheaper' entails (1) better products at the same price, (2) products of the same quality at a cheaper price, (3) new products not currently available and (4) better products at a cheaper price than those currently available. The competitive strategies of individual companies can be very different depending on which of these alternatives they choose to differentiate their products.

It goes without saying that the most effective way to survive and gain market share is to pursue the fourth strategy, and it was precisely this strategy that many large Japanese companies adopted in the postwar period in the international market for manufactured goods. Hereafter the competitive strategy adopted by these Japanese companies will be called the 'better and cheaper' strategy.

One of the reasons why Japan was able to achieve phenomenal economic growth and development after the Second World War was that the open market welcomed better products at cheaper prices. At the same time this market was very important to Japan as a source of raw materials and basic or advanced technology and machinery.

'Better and cheaper' is, however, at best only a necessary condition for companies to prosper in the central marketplace. That is, just competing by the rule of 'better and cheaper' will lead to dog-eat-dog competition. Charity organisation and government-owned companies might enter the competition for objectives other than profit maximisation. Or existing companies might collude temporarily to pursue the 'better and cheaper' strategy, disregarding profitability in an attempt to shut out new entrants. In this case, new entrants that could have brought better and/or cheaper products, ideas or technology to the marketplace are prevented from making a positive contribution to the market. Furthermore, the existing companies will fall into so-called overcompetition, and will have idle capacity and operate in the red, leading to a waste of capital and other resources. Therefore the pursuit of 'better and cheaper' will not always lead to the optimal allocation of resources for the system as a whole.

In the central marketplace there is another important rule of competition imposed from the capital market side: companies are required to achieve a certain minimum return on invested capital. This minimum acceptable return corresponds to the cost of capital (to be dealt with in depth in Part III), which constitutes the hurdle or minimum acceptable rate in the competition for 'better and cheaper'. Only when companies have met these two conditions can they be considered to be creating useful economic value.

The interest rate prevailing in the debt capital market is shown by i, in Figure 2.1, and the providers of debt capital will give the company management a pass mark only if the company earns enough return on capital to pay the interest on the debt capital provided at the beginning of the cycle. In other words, the management is expected to increase D to at least $(1 + i) \times D$. Similarly the providers of equity capital, E, will require the company to realise at least r, the minimum acceptable return on equity capital for a pass mark to be awarded to the management. In other words, the shareholders expect the company management to increase E to at least $(1 + r) \times E$ by the end of the fiscal year.

The reason for showing companies as a 'black box' for increasing capital, (see also chapter 4, section 4.3.1), is that measuring a company's value-creation capability becomes very difficult for outside investors as the business operations become more and more complicated and sophisticated. When the business is simple and all its competitors are producing similar products with a similar mix of capital, technology and labour and selling at similar prices, we may be able to judge the company's capability by comparing such operating measures as the amount of capital stock per employee, sales per employee or number of products produced per employee.

However, should the combination of capital and labour vary, or different technologies be involved to produce different types of products to be sold at different prices, such simple operational measures will not be able to determine whether or not the companies are actually creating value, or which company is superior or inferior to others. There may be companies that, no matter how hard they work or how useful their products or services are, simply waste capital. In order to judge the total performance of the value-creation activities of companies in a objective manner, there is no other way than to measure it by the productivity of capital, or by the return on capital employed, since capital is the ultimate measure of value and value creation.

In this sense the primary means of evaluating value creation for outside investors is to evaluate the company's financial performance. After all, capitalism evaluates any economic activity by the productivity of capital in general, and of risk or equity capital in particular, because economic value creation starts with an injection of risk capital and ends with the recovery of it.

What, then should be the behaviour of those company managers who are judged under such a paradigm? First of all, from the point of view of company managers capital is as necessary a resource as raw materials and labour. In the central marketplace, capital is available at a price that reflects the degree of safety or attractiveness of the borrower. In this sense it is necessary to have a well-developed and efficient capital market, as will be explained later. In such a capital market, it is assumed that fair prices for various types of capital will be constantly quoted, reflecting demand and supply with a particular mix of expected risk and return.

The primary responsibility of corporate managers is to earn as much return as possible on top of the cost or a minimum acceptable rate of return on capital required by the market. Fair prices or costs of *D* and *E* are set by the numerous investors who participate in the capital market. Company managers are only price takers in that sense: the most they can do is to choose a particular mix of *D* and *E*, or capital structure.

2.3 RULES FOR EVALUATING COMPANY PERFORMANCE

As explained in the previous section, the value-creation activities of companies in the central marketplace will ultimately be evaluated by the productivity of capital or the return on capital employed. In this simplified diagram, by definition D is capital with a fixed return, and no matter how much total capital, $D + E$, may increase, the reward that is paid to the suppliers of D is fixed at i by the contract. As a result the ultimate criterion of the performance of company managers is the return on shareholders' capital or equity. This is exactly what is meant by the maximisation of shareholders' wealth being the primary objective of investor-owned companies.

Put another way, the capital market evaluates the ability of individual companies to create economic value through stock prices. The stock market does this by discounting expected future cash flows with the required or minimum acceptable return, r, encouraging company managers to use r as the hurdle rate when they make decisions on new investment expenditure. The book return on equity (ROE) is the return on the average historical value of shareholders' capital. Consider a situation in which investors expect at least a 10 per cent (post-tax) return on their capital. In this case the minimum acceptable ROE will be 10 per cent. However there is no guarantee that the company concerned will be able to attain a 10 per cent ROE.

Suppose a company is so well managed that it is expected to continue to realise an average 20 per cent return in future, and consider how the market will evaluate this company. If we assume for the time being that this company is of average risk, the stock market will value it by raising the stock price to the level at which the company can expect to realise the 10 per cent minimum acceptable return in future. In this case the stock price of the company with the expected ROE of 20 per cent will increase to twice its book value in the market, making the price-to-book-value ratio to two to one.

Conversely, if there is a company whose expected ROE is only 5 per cent, the market will value this company by decreasing the stock price until the expected return – based on the current stock price – corresponds to 10 per cent, or to half the book value. In this way the stock market is valuing the ability of an individual company to produce a return on shareholders' capital on a daily basis through collective voting by numerous investors in the stock market. As soon as the market's expectation of a company's future outlook changes, the stock price of the company will change accordingly.

Ultimately the stock market is where a value is placed on the ability of companies to use shareholders' capital productively, or their ability to generate a cash flow, as will be explained later. The fact that the evaluation of companies in the central marketplace is directly linked to stock prices means that the system gives incentives and punishments to managers through stock price changes in the market.

As a result, because of the way the central marketplace is designed, the system as a whole is strongly biassed towards encouraging risk taking by company managers. Since managers are rewarded for high capital productivity, as measured by ROE, competition among companies is bound to be aimed at high returns. However, if the market for goods and services is very competitive and open to new entrants, a business opportunity that promises a high return at low risk will not last very long.

Should such a niche exist, sooner or later, there will be new entrants and the return will reduce to a level that matches the risk, so that managers aiming for a high return will have to take a greater risk. If a company wants to be rewarded highly in the market, it must risk trying something unique or innovative that no one else is doing at the moment. Likewise the system offers a strong incentive to develop epoch-making new technologies. The type of management that incrementally improves existing technologies or products is not valued very highly in this system. For this reason, in contrast with Japanese companies, the business strategies of US companies tend to be unique and emphasise differentiation of their products from those of their competitors.

Because of the above, in the central marketplace there is little incentive to pursue a 'better and cheaper' strategy if it ends up with a low return on capital, even though it may be very effective in terms of survival and increased market share.

As a resource allocation system, the most prominent characteristic of US capitalism is that it incorporates a strong incentive to take risks. Socialist centrally planned economies and many market-based economies, including Japan, try to avoid the risk of scarce resources being wasted through trial and error in the open market. Among the major nations, only the United States has developed a system that encourages risk taking by offering economic or financial incentives. Because of this the United States has been able to function as the central marketplace of the entire capitalist market economy.

The main reason why the capitalist market economy has succeeded while the socialist centrally planned economy has failed is that the former has mechanisms to encourage and motivate a vast number of the public to start their own businesses and bring new ideas, products and technology to the marketplace. Not all nations, including Japan, have to adopt a similar system as the fruits are on offer in the World market at fair prices. It is even possible for the purchasers of products to improve them and bring them back to the market with higher added value.

Of course it can be very costly to run such a central marketplace. For example, in order to encourage business managers to engage in new and uncertain business opportunities, the market has to provide attractive financial rewards for success. Likewise, in order to encourage investors to provide risk capital for such ventures, the market has to provide a sufficiently high return to justify such investment. In addition a large amount of equity capital is necessary to cushion risk if debt capital is to be raised at a reasonable cost.

In the central marketplace it is not assumed, as has been the case in Japan, that any company or any industry, once started, will last forever. Rather the system helps companies with high capital productivity to prosper, and companies with low capital productivity to be taken over by those that can make better use of investors' money.

3 The Role of the Capital Market

3.1 CASH FLOW AS THE SOURCE OF VALUE

In managing US capitalism, which aims for optimum resource allocation through numerous investor-owned companies, the role of the capital market is critical because it monitors the performance of companies, evaluates them and encourages or discourages their growth. In this respect, the role of the stock market is especially important. Metaphorically speaking, the stock market is the supreme court of value-creation activities in the central marketplace. As will be explained later, the capital market sets prices on various pieces of debt and equity capital, which are slices of the total cash flow generated by companies and reflect the expected return and risk. In other words, the capital market sets the cost of various pieces of capital. Companies pursue their value-creation activities by using the average cost of capital set by the market as the hurdle rates for their investment decisions.

The 'cash flow' is used as the common measure of value creation by companies in the central marketplace. We will look at the concept of valuation based on cash flow using the simplified example in Figure 3.1.

For simplificify, we shall consider a project that is to be completed in five years. If, in the beginning, 100 currency units are invested in the project, it is expected that the project will bring net cash flows of 25, 35, 15, 40 and 50 units in the first, second, third, fourth and fifth years respectively. Let us calculate the expected return of the entire project. The rate of return that equate the sum of the present values of the

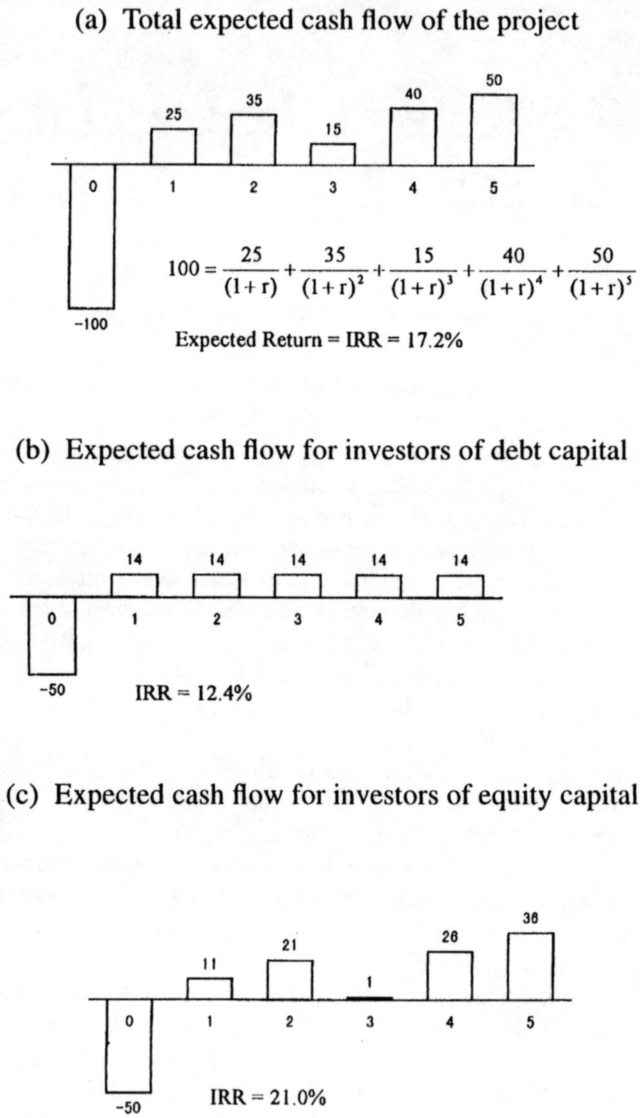

FIGURE 3.1 Value creation and valuation: (1) a five-year project

expected future cash flow and the initial investment of 100 units is the expected rate of return, or IRR (internal rate of return) of the project. In this case it is 17.2 per cent.

However, this is the expected return on the project if it is financed from a single source. In reality companies finance part of their investment, say 50 per cent, with fixed-interest debt and the rest with risk or equity capital. There are many different debt repayment patterns, but to keep things simple let's assume that the company makes five equal or level payments of 14 at the end of each year to serve principal and interest. For the providers of the debt capital the expected annual return is 12.4 per cent. The residual cash flow will belong to the providers of the risk capital, or stockholders, and for them the expected annual return is 21 per cent.

Now, can we say whether the expected return on the equity capital is too high, too low or appropriate compared with that for debt capital? The answer is not obvious, because we have to take into consideration the difference in risk born by the providers of debt and equity.

In the first place, the cash flow for the project as a whole is simply a best estimate or the expected value, and there is no guarantee at all. Moreover, since the fixed charge is included in the capital structure, the expected cash flow to the stockholders, who only have a residual claim, becomes even more uncertain and risky. Therefore the expected return for equity holders should be higher than the interest charge.

The adequate rate of expected return or the risk premium over and above the interest rate, taking into account the risk, will depend on the risk preference of the equity providers. However, in a well-developed capital market with a large number of well-trained, rational investors, we can assumed that the interest rate and stock prices will reflect the degree of risk and the average risk preference of the investors.

Accordingly, in a well-developed and efficient capital market, the investors will collectively decide a price for both the debt and the equity portion of the package at which they all feel fairly treated. And if the market participants still think that the return to the stockholders is unreasonably high, after taking risk into proper consideration, a massive arbitrage will take place and equilibrium prices for both debt and equity will be established in terms of the expected return.

Companies with a good financial performance will enjoy favourable credit and bond ratings, as well as a high valuation in the stock market, which will enable them to raise capital at favourable terms for further growth. Conversely, companies with a poor financial performance will be handicapped in their attempt to raise debt and equity capital, and will be discouraged from growing.

3.2 EVALUATION OF A COMPANY AS A GOING CONCERN

A company whose stock is listed on the stock exchange is different from a project with a finite life. It is assumed to be a going concern and is expected to continue its business indefinitely. A going concern may have numerous projects of finite duration so some adjustments have to be made, including a depreciation allowance for reinvesting part of recovered capital to perpetuate the current operation. These factors complicate the situation, but the principle of valuing the performance of companies is essentially the same as that for a single project. Figure 3.2 shows this in a simplified form.

As shown in Figure 3.2a, the company is expected to continue to generate a certain amount of operating cash flow each year. We will assume that the company's capital structure is 50 per cent fixed-cost debt capital and 50 per cent equity capital. We will also assume, as the extreme case, that the company has only consol-type bonds outstanding and will continue to pay a fixed coupon, C, indefinitely (as shown in Figure 3.2b). Out of the total operating cash flow generated by this company, all the residual cash flow – after subtracting interest C, to be paid to the holders of consol – goes to the stockholders (shown in Figure 3.2c as CF_1, CF_2 ...)

The theoretical price of the consol (B) is the sum of the present values of the infinite flow of C discounted at the

(a) Total operating cash flow (= after-tax income + depreciation + interest charges – required new investment)

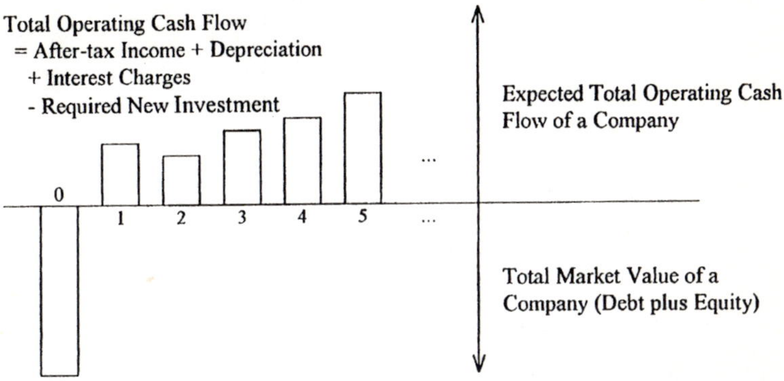

(b) Stake for debt holders

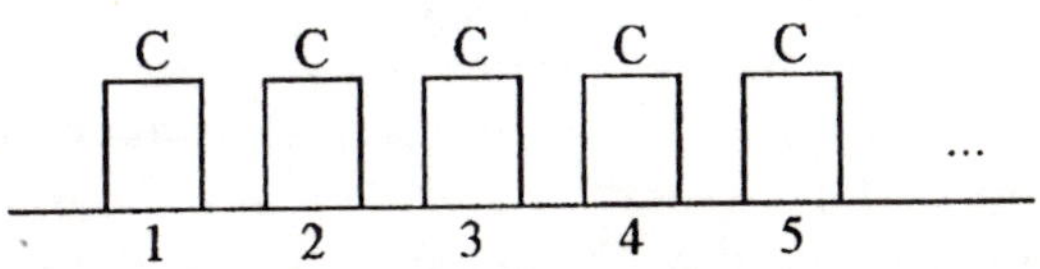

$$B_0 = \frac{C}{(1+i)} + \frac{C}{(1+i)^2} + \frac{C}{(1+i)^3} + \ldots = \frac{C}{i}$$

FIGURE 3.2 Value creation and valuation: (2) going concern

(c) Stake for shareholders

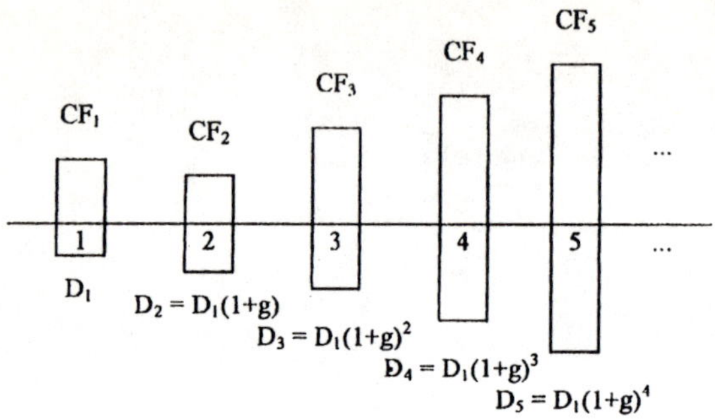

$$P_0 = \frac{CF_1}{(1+r)} + \frac{CF_2}{(1+r)^2} + \frac{CF_3}{(1+r)^3} + \ldots$$

$$= \frac{D_1}{(1+r)} + \frac{D_1(1+g)}{(1+r)^2} + \frac{D_1(1+g)^2}{(1+r)^3} + \ldots = \frac{D_1}{r-g}$$

where $D_t = D_{t-1x}(1+g)$

FIGURE 3.2 Continued

appropriate interest rate, *i*, expected by the investors. This value is given in arithmetical terms by *C*/*i*.

The theoretical price of the stock, *P*, is shown in Figure 3.2c. If the investors' average expected return on this stock is set at *r* in the market, the theoretical price of the stock can be calculated as shown. It is also possible to estimate the investors' average expected return from the current stock price and the expected value of future cash flows.

Under modern US capitalism – which is characterised by a clear separation between ownership and management of large companies – investors, who are basically outsiders, primarily base their evaluation of companies on public information. The task of accurately forecasting the long-term expected cash flow is not easy even for well-trained and well-informed professional analysts and there is a need to make the valuation process a little easier. One way to do this is to base the valuation of the company on the expected flow of dividends.

Dividends are essentially a partial, periodic redemption of shareholders' equity ownership, drawn from the operating cash flow. The main reason why investors invest in stocks that bear a residual risk is that they expect them to offer higher returns than risk-free financial assets. Accordingly, if the investors have full trust in the company management, they should leave all the cash flow with the company for further investment, as long as the company has attractive business opportunities.

However under modern US capitalism, in which investors are mostly outsiders interested only in financial return and therefore frequently buy and sell stocks in the secondary market, it is difficult for investors to have such complete trust in the company management. Therefore, as credible evidence that the company is well managed, part of the fruits of its operation are periodically paid out in the form of dividends.

The ultimate source of the value of the stock is the cash flow, *CF*, which belongs to shareholders (as shown in Figure 3.2c), not the dividend. Accordingly it can not be said unconditionally that a short-term increase in dividends is a positive factor for the stock price, because it may mean reduced reinvestment opportunities and reduced cash flows in the future. But if we look at the entire life of the company, the sum of the discounted present value of all the cash flows above the line in Figure 3.2c should in principle coincide with that of all the dividends, *D*, below the line. In this sense we can estimate the theoretical value of the stock as the sum of the properly discounted present values of all future dividends. This is called a dividend discount model, or DDM.

Even with this model we have to forecast the flow of dividend for all future years, which is not easy. Therefore another simplification is often made. As a means of estimating the dividend streams in the long term it is assumed that annual dividends will increase at a constant growth rate, *g*, and by estimating that single growth rate we can reduce the general dividend discount model to what is called a constant growth rate model. In this simplified version, as shown under Figure 3.2c, the theoretical stock value is $P_0 = D_1/(r - g)$. Here D_1 is the expected dividend per share in period one, g is the expected growth rate of dividend, and r is the expected return that the investors currently expect from investing in the stock of the company. Here, r is assumed to be greater than g.

Finally, the PER, or price–earnings ratio, the most commonly used measure of the stock valuation, can be easily deduced from the constant growth version of the dividend discount model.

In order to relate the stock price to after-tax profit per share, the most readily available profit number, we divide both sides of the theoretical stock price equation ($P_0 = D_1/[r - g]$) by the expected value of earning per share E_1. Then the equation can be rewritten as follows:

$$P_0 / E_1 = (D_1 / E_1)/(r - g)$$

In other words, the price–earnings ratio is defined as: (expected value of dividend payout ratio)/(investors' expected return – expected growth rate).

3.3 DIVERSIFICATION OF THE SOURCE OF CAPITAL THROUGH 'SLICING' THE TOTAL CASH FLOW

So far I have simplified the company's capital structure to consist of just two types of capital, namely debt and equity capital. This means that the claim on the company's total cash flow is divided between two groups of investors with different claims, as shown in Figure 3.3a.

In reality, any large investor-owned company raises capital from much more diverse sources by capitalising its operating cash flow. Companies try to make the best use of their operating cash flow to attract capital in such a way as to maximise their market value in the capital market. In order to achieve this goal, they slice the operating cash flow into many pieces

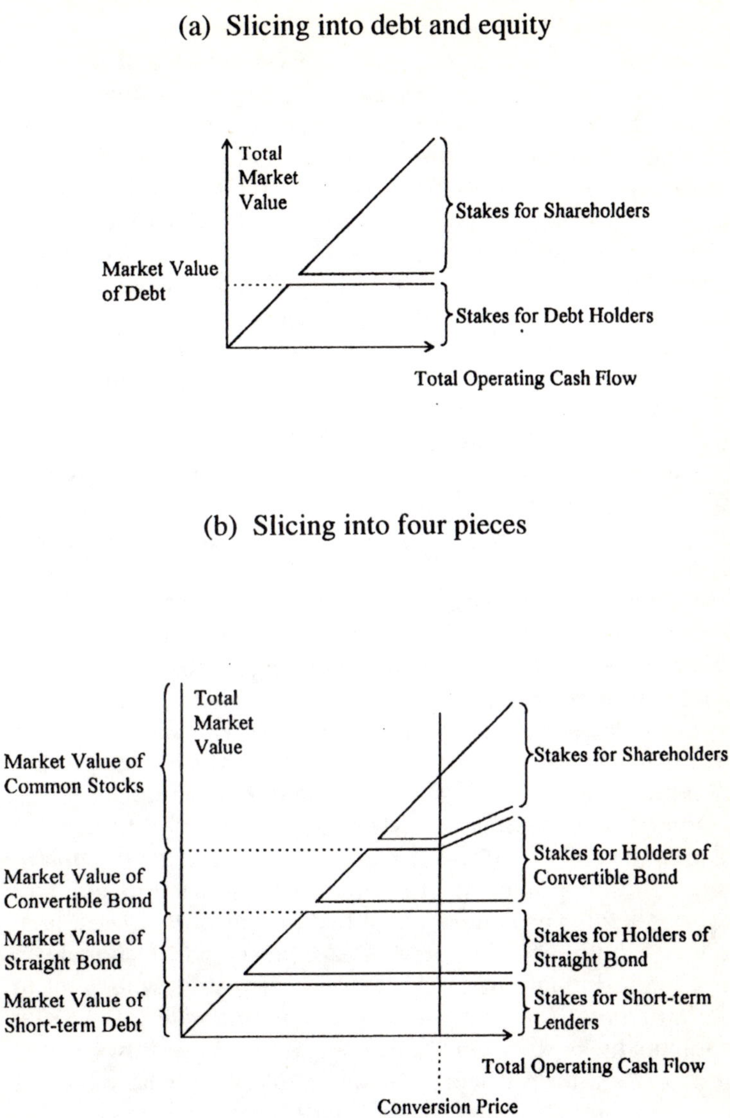

FIGURE 3.3 Slicing the total operating cash flow

this goal, they slice the operating cash flow into many pieces and 'retail' the slices as a different mix of return and risk.

If we look at the securities issued by large companies today, we will be surprised to find how diverse they are. There are hundreds of different securities in terms of patterns of interest payment, convertibility into stocks and so on. The logic behind the efforts to divide cash flow in ways that will appeal to the special needs of groups of investors is that, if the companies can provide exactly the slice of cash flow required by investors who are interested only in a certain fraction of the total cash flow that has a particular return–risk feature, then the investors will pay something extra for that effort. If the company managers are successful in this, then the total value of the company in the capital market will increase. Figure 3.3b shows how a company slices its operating cash flow into four pieces and sells them to suppliers of short-term debt, straight corporate bonds, convertible bonds and common stock.

In a well-developed capital market, many different pieces of cash flow with different return–risk characteristics are efficiently priced and change hands every day. In order to match the diverse needs of both investors and borrowers to the maximum degree at minimum cost, a well-functioning or 'efficient' capital market (as described in the next chapter) is imperative for the smooth functioning of US capitalism.

Diversification of sources of capital by companies also leads to the creation of diverse groups of investors with potentially conflicting interests. For investors who want to avoid all risk, companies provide a 'slice' that promises the lowest possible risk but also a low return, as represented by short-term bank loans and commercial paper. For investors who want to commit capital for a longer term but do not wish to take any major business risk, companies sell future cash flows in the form of long-term bonds. For those investors who expect a much higher return and are willing to accept the associated risk, companies 'sell' all the residual cash flow that remains after the payments to all senior claims are made in the form of common stocks.

The rights to the various pieces of cash flow are nothing but financial contracts specifying who will receive how much, in what order and under what conditions. There will be no conflict as long as the company meets all its obligations, but should the business suffer financial distress the various claim holders will experience a conflict of interest: rather than cooperating with each other to help the company to overcome its problems, they may fight among themselves to secure their share of the operating cash flow.

It is therefore important for companies to build a relationship of trust with their various stakeholders and investors in order to manage the multilateral relationship between them. Only then will they be able fully to enjoy the rewards of diversifying their sources of capital. When companies fail adequately to manage this situation, then the issue of 'agency cost' starts to become serious and may cancel or even outweigh the benefits of diversification.

Accordingly, a major challenge for the management of the central capital market is to satisfy the diverse needs of investors and borrowers, while at the same time keeping agency costs at a reasonable level. This is where the idea of an efficient capital market comes in. In Chapter 4 we will look into this issue in the case of common stock.

4 The Stock Market as the Final Judge of the Value-Creation Process

4.1 TWO APPROACHES TO STOCK VALUATION: TECHNICAL VS FUNDAMENTAL ANALYSIS

Two approaches have traditionally coexisted for analysing stock prices and making investment decisions. One school holds that stock prices are nothing but a 'castle in the air' without any solid foundation, and that market movements are essentially the repeated development and bursting of 'bubbles' of investor sentiments in response to the mass psychology of the market. The other school holds that stocks, like any other asset, have a fundamental economic value that reflects investors' expectations of future cash flows, and that a stock's price is determined daily by investors' collective decisions about the stock's reasonable investment value. The former is called the 'castle in the air' school (or the 'bubble' school), and the latter the 'fundamental value' school.

The notion that stock prices will rise when everyone thinks they will (or fall when everyone thinks they will fall) has strong supporters in markets throughout the world. It is possible to describe the stock market movements in Japan and the United States during the 1980s as the repeated development and bursting of bubbles – a phenomenon not too different in nature from the tulip speculation in seventeenth-century Holland, the speculative South Sea Bubble boom in eighteenth-century Britain, and the phenomenal escalation in US stock prices during the 1920s.

The intellectual leadership of the castle in the air school of thinking was provided by John Maynard Keynes, the famed economist who likened stock investments to 'beauty contests' in his *General Theory of Employment, Interest and Money*.[1] Comparing stocks to the beauty contests that the London tabloid newspapers of his day featured to boost their circulation, Keynes stated that stock price formation is essentially a 'third, fourth or fifth degree exercise' that represents the collective guesswork of the crowds on what average opinion expects the average opinion to be. In short, Keynes held that, in the absence of well-founded and reliable information, rigorous theories or clear criteria, stock prices are the result of nothing but mass psychology. The investment approach that is consistent with this reasoning is the technical analysis practised by chartists.

In contrast the fundamental value school maintains that each share of the stock of a company embodies a claim on the residual value of the company's cash flow, and like any other asset it clearly has an intrinsic or fundamental value as an investment. This value exists in the company's 'fundamentals', which include the company's assets, its cash flow, profits and dividends, and the consensus of market participants on this value is what determines the price of the stock. The investment technique that is consistent with this approach is known as fundamental analysis, as practised by security analysts.

The intellectual leader of the fundamental value school was Benjamin Graham, whose techniques of security analysis called for careful analysis of the financial statements and financial performance of companies, estimating the fundamental value of a stock and comparing it with the stock's market price – thereby identifying undervalued and overvalued stocks.[2]

Does the fundamental value school think that stock prices basically reflect fundamental values? The answer is no. Sidney Cottle carefully spelled out the position of the fundamental value school:

> The fact that the market is almost always wrong and that there is consistently a gap between the market price and the fundamental value is the very reason we securities analysts exist. Because the market consensus is almost always wrong, we can achieve good investment performance through the efforts of careful securities analysis. Even though we sometimes make mistakes, we do considerably better than the market.[3]

In this sense the castle in the air and the fundamental value schools are not necessarily incompatible with each other. One way of differentiating between the two schools is that, whereas the former pursues 'changes' in near-term prices, the latter seeks 'something that doesn't change' (intrinsic value). Another distinction is that, whereas the former attaches great importance to 'when to buy' (timing), the latter stresses 'what to buy' (stock selection). Even so the two schools have largely coexisted, and no assertion can be made as to which one is correct or better. They were, in fact, both widely used by practitioners to supplement each other until the validity of both schools was challenged by modern portfolio theory.

4.2 MODERN PORTFOLIO THEORY

Modern portfolio theory (MPT), which systematised the securities investment process into an academic science, developed mainly out of the intellectual pursuits of scholars after the Second World War. Because of the nature of the subject, MPT is highly interdisciplinary in scope and has benefited from the contributions of scholars in many fields, including traditional economists such as Samuelson and Tobin, monetary economists such as Fama and Miller, operations research/statistics/management scientists such as Markowitz and Sharpe, game theorists such as Morgenstern and physicists such as Osborne, as well as various mathematicians and, more recently, rocket scientists. Moreover, as during its early stages portfolio theory was developed totally independently of practitioners, the ideas were both free and unrestrained, and led to the entire range of traditional investment theories and practices being reexamined from a totally new perspective. In this process, both technical analysis and fundamental analysis provided rich samples for these scholars to test various hypotheses.

While MPT is a multifaceted body of theory, hypotheses and techniques, one of its key pillars is equilibrium theory, as represented by the capital asset pricing model (CAPM) and the arbitrage pricing theory (APT). MPT assumes the existence of an equilibrium price for securities, and in this sense it stands on the side of the fundamental value school in the traditional dichotomy. However, while traditional security analysis aims at estimating justifiable stock prices, MPT focuses on the equilibrium of expected returns implicit in stock prices.

Another pillar of MPT is the efficient market hypothesis. In a well-developed capital market like the one in the United States, investors, including institutions, are primarily interested in financial returns as opposed to relationships. They are also risk averse and outsiders in terms of fundamental corporate information. They primarily base their investment decisions on public information. Under such circumstances a stock price changes mainly in response to new information that affects expectations about the company's future cash flows and its discount rate. Accordingly, MPT places great importance on how such investment information is reflected in the price. When new information is promptly and properly incorporated into stock pricing, the market is considered to be efficient. In contrast, inefficient markets are those in which stock prices do not promptly and properly reflect new information.

Scholars have used a variety of approaches when carrying out research on the efficiency of the market. A common theme in all these studies is the attempt to determine whether investment decisions that actively apply specific information, specific methods or strategies consistently and significantly outperform passive approaches such as mechanically investing in market indexes.

For purposes of convenience, the efficient market hypothesis is tested in three forms – 'weak', 'semi-strong' and 'strong' – according to the type of information that is subject to verification.[4] Under this classification, the point at issue is the validity of investment information acquired through technical analysis in the weak form, and through traditional fundamental analysis in the semi-strong form. In the case of strong market efficiency, the issue becomes the validity of all investment information, even including illegal insider information, and investment strategies used by experts who manage mutual funds or pensions.

While many analyses have been carried out concerning the validity of investment information for the three levels, the tentative conclusion to date suggests the following:

1. To date no superiority has been observed for investment strategies based on information on past stock prices and volumes (considered important in technical analysis) when compared with passive management after transaction fees are subtracted.
2. Similarly, no superiority has been observed for investment strategies based on publicly available information on company profits, dividends and so on (considered important in traditional security analysis) when compared with passive investment.
3. The validity of information possessed by exchange floor specialists and insider information cannot be completely denied.

As a result of these studies, it has become generally recognised that stock markets, such as those in the United States, where the bulk of investment decision making rests with professional institutional investors who act as fiduciaries for other people's money, are sufficiently efficient in both the weak and semi-strong forms of the efficient market hypothesis, although some inefficiencies remain in the strong form. In this respect MPT can be viewed as a study of both active and passive investment in a nearly efficient market.[5]

4.3 CONDITIONS FOR EFFICIENT STOCK PRICE FORMATION

Common stocks are financial instruments that confer both ownership rights to the residual corporate cash flow and voting rights or corporate control. The castle in the air school, the fundamental value school and MPT all view stocks as financial assets primarily for investment or speculative purposes. In short, these investment theories all attach importance to the cash flow aspect of stocks. Therefore the main argument is whether a stock price appropriately reflects market participants'[2] best estimates of the expected value of future discounted cash flow.

Rarely, though, has efficient stock price formation been a norm in any market, as envisioned by MPT. The US stock market since the 1970s is considered a rare exception. There are, of course, many good reasons for MPT to have blossomed in the United States. Based on the US experience, the following section considers the necessary conditions for stock prices to be efficiently or nearly efficiently formed on a basis that generally and reasonably reflects fundamental value.

The term efficiency can be defined in many ways. Here we borrow the explanation of William Sharpe, who is one of the founding fathers of MPT, because of his concept of the β coefficient and CAPM. In one of his books on investment, he defines market efficiency in the following manner:

> Imagine a world in which (1) all investors have costless access to currently available information about the future; (2) all investors are good analysts; and (3) all investors pay close attention to market prices and adjust their holdings appropriately. In such a market, a security's price will be a good estimate of its *investment value*, where investment value is the present value of the security's future prospects as estimated by well-informed and capable analysts.

An *efficient market* can now be defined:

> A (perfectly) efficient market is one in which every security's price equals its investment value at all times.
>
> As mentioned earlier, in an efficient market, a security's price will be a good estimate of its investment value, where investment value is the present value of the security's future prospects as estimated by well-informed and capable analysts. Any substantial disparity between price and value would reflect market inefficiency. In a well-developed and free market, major inefficiencies are rare. The reason is not hard to find. Major disparities between price and investment value will be noted by alert analysts, who will seek to take advantages of their discoveries. Securities priced below value (known as underpriced or undervalued securities) will be purchased, creating pressure for price increases due to the increased demand to buy. Securities priced above value (known as overpriced or overvalued securities) will be sold, creating pressure for price decreases due to the increased supply to sell. As investors seek to take advantages of opportunities created by temporary inefficiencies, they will cause the inefficiencies to be reduced, denying the less alert and the less informed a chance to obtain large abnormal profits.[6]

What are the necessary social, economic and business conditions that will bring about the efficient pricing of stocks, as defined by Sharpe? Or, what will it take for the majority of investors to behave in such ways as Sharpe characterises when he defines market efficiency? If we observe past development' in the United States, we can point out the following factors.

4.3.1 Companies as 'Black Boxes' to Increase Capital

In an economy where investors motivated purely by financial return are the driving force of stock investments, investor-owned companies are regarded primarily as enigmatic 'black boxes' that are expected to increase the investors' capital. In such an environment a company can justify its existence only by continuing to demonstrate, through the creation of cash flows, a financial performance that satisfies the expectations of the aggregate of investors that comprise the capital market. Unless it can generate reasonable profits (cash flows) it will be evaluated as a waste of other people's capital, no matter how useful its products or services. It is this concept of a company that serves as a major premise for efficient stock price formation.

Consequently, in a well-functioning capital market such as that in the United States, investors constantly monitor the financial performance of companies – and constantly adjust cash flow forecasts – to estimate a reasonable value for stocks. It is the combination of these numerous estimates that determines, at any point in time, the price of stocks. If there is an increase in the expected future cash flow, the efficient market will immediately reflect these higher expectations and the stock price will rise to a point that reflects the discounted present value of the new expected cash flow.

4.3.2 Separation of Ownership and Management

Another condition for efficient stock price formation is that the majority of investors are motivated to maximise their financial returns, properly adjusted according to risk. In the early stages of a company's development, the entrepreneur typically invests his or her own capital and/or mobilises the capital of friends and relatives to carry out the business. During this early stage, ownership and management are almost always identical or in full agreement. As the business gains success and expands in scale, however, an increasing need for new capital leads most companies to offer stock to the general public. As the business further expands and its operations become more sophisticated and complex, management is often entrusted to a specially trained group of professional managers. As a result the management and ownership of most large companies today are largely, if not completely, separated. Indeed Alfred Chandler suggested that the emergence of large investor-owned companies, led by professional managers, was one of the most important factors behind modern industrial development.[7]

When these stages of company development are viewed historically for various countries, we see that the requisite conditions were realised in the United States during the 1920s and in Japan during the years between the end of the Second World War and the period of high economic growth (1945–1970). In both cases, even though the combined mass of general investors are the true owners of companies, they are fragmented, isolated and powerless as individuals. They have little chance to participate actively in the company's management, and as outsiders they generally confine their interest to the return on their investments.

While some of these investors may be long-term, stable shareholders, this is not necessarily the case because usually there exists a reasonably well-developed secondary market. Consequently, whenever necessary, investment returns can be realised by selling stocks in the secondary market. For these investors, whether to hold on to certain stocks or sell them at the current prices becomes a daily concern. These investors typically have access only to public information about the company. Individual investors have little impact on the market price as they are basically 'price takers', confined to buying or selling at prices established by the market.

4.3.3 The Growing Fiduciary Role of Institutional Investors

A third condition for efficient stock price formation is the institutionalisation of stock investment. Just as ownership and management are fully separated in well-developed market economies, the ownership of financial assets is clearly separated from the functions of investment decision making and portfolio management with respect to stock investment. This requires a large number of professionals to manage assets on behalf of or at the request of citizens. This is what is meant by the 'institutionalisation' of stock investment.

The institutionalisation process started to make rapid strides in the US stock markets during the 1960s. For some three decades after the Great Depression, throughout the Second World War and through to the 1950s, the United States experienced a period of severe deflation, low growth and low interest rates, all of which tended to foster an ultraconservative approach to stock investment. With the coming of the 1960s, however, optimism and bullishness took hold, and during the 'Golden Sixties' an unprecedented boom occurred in stock investment. This boom was carried on the shoulders of mutual funds – especially the 'go–go' funds, which stressed short-term capital gains through intensive investment in growth stocks.

Also, corporate pension funds steadily grew throughout the 1960s, becoming the largest investors in the stock market by the end of the decade. As a result these institutional investors became the driving force of the stock market, their share of trading volume doubling in the 1960s from one third to two thirds of the total market volume by the end of the decade.

Institutional investors essentially function like conduits – a term that is sometimes applied to them. Apart from fees and commissions, all assets under management and the gains from investment belong to the ultimate beneficiaries or owners of the assets. In professionally managing the assets entrusted to them, the managers of these institutions serve as agents or fiduciaries for the citizens. (It should be noted here that institutional investors of this sort are quite different from the so-called corporate investors, including banks, in Japan.)

These activities are widely understood to be subject to the rules that govern the principal–agent relationship under British and US common law, and are also governed by the criterion of fiduciary responsibility. Professional investment managers in the United States are further bound by the prudent-man rule, as established by the courts.

The management of corporate pensions, most of which are entrusted to outside fund managers, involves standards that are typical of those imposed on US investment managers. The activities and evaluation methods of corporate pension managers are strictly regulated by the Employee Retirement Income Security Act (ERISA), which obliges such managers to observe the standards embodied in the concept of fiduciary responsibility and the prudent-man rule. The former requires that the fiduciaries of a fund act solely for the benefit of the principals in all their decisions, while the latter requires that all actions follow the same common sense that a prudent investor would use in managing his or her own assets. While both these principles are somewhat abstract, they nevertheless subject fund managers to legal action for unjustified investment decisions or unprofessional conduct that exposes the principals to losses.

As a general rule, these standards of conduct apply not only to the management of corporate pensions, but also to all other institutional investors such as trust banks, life insurance companies and investment trusts. As a result, stock investors in the United States are not usually in a position to make a long-term commitment to the development and growth of companies. Instead they merely buy and sell shares based on their evaluation of companies as 'black boxes' generating cash flows in the capacity of neutral, arm's-length, third-party investors.

4.3.4 The Importance of Performance Competition

The results of an investment – or its performance – can be measured by the total return on market price over a given time period (for example three months or a year). The concept of evaluating investment performance is also one of the central themes of MPT, and the procedure of measuring performance has made remarkable progress under MPT. As in the case of verifying the efficient market hypothesis, MPT focuses on how to measure and evaluate objectively and logically whether fund managers have actually achieved a superior performance. In other words, MPT attempts to measure precisely the extent of risks taken and returns achieved.

According to the capital asset pricing model (CAPM), an efficient market determines prices so as to provide, on a long-term average basis, returns that rise in proportion to the β risk relative to the market. In other words, CAPM holds that an efficient market should reward only systematic risks reflected in β coefficients – not the specific risks of individual stocks – a strong rationale is required to justify the taking of specific risks arising from factors inherent to particular stocks. Any manager who unsuccessfully takes such specific risks will receive a negative evaluation as a matter of course.

In addition, MPT attempts to distinguish whether good performance is merely due to a favourable market environment and good luck, or to good timing and superior skills in selecting sectors, business groups or particular issues. One method used in this process is performance factor analysis; another is the evaluation of long-term average performance over periods of 5–10 years. Today many US companies employ performance evaluation firms to collect data on the results of the investment advisors and managers handling their pension funds, and to provide summaries that analyse and rank the results of hundreds of outside managers.

How does performance competition lead to efficient price formation? First, because it is difficult for fund managers to take indiscriminate risks in a comparative setting, it is difficult to play the market in total disregard of whether stocks are undervalued or overvalued in terms of fundamentals. Fundamental values thus become the main basis for active fund management that depends on judgment as to which stocks are underpriced or overpriced.

Moreover the performance of institutional portfolio managers is usually monitored with respect to the overall results of large-scale portfolios rather than stock selections. Even if managers are successful in one stock at some stage, they can still lose out to passively managed index funds if the stock is not sold at the proper time and replaced by another with an attractive investment prospect. Because of this, a systematic approach based on logical price judgments in accordance with fundamental values is indispensable.

Accordingly, the individual actions of innumerable investment managers – all competing fiercely to achieve higher returns – are the foundation upon which an efficient market stands. That is, a large number of professionals are always watching for non-efficient segments of the market, and will immediately buy any security that is underpriced relative to its fundamental value. Likewise any issue that has become even slightly overpriced will immediately be sold, as all managers realises that their performance will be negatively affected if they carelessly hold on to overvalued stock while other managers are selling it.

Stock prices tend to reflect fundamental values properly and promptly when the majority of investors compete according to the rule of immediately buying undervalued stocks and selling overvalued ones.

4.3.5 The Relationship between Shareholders and Companies

In a market where the above conditions hold, the relationship between the investors in a stock and the issuing company inevitably becomes a 'spot' or temporary one. Table 6.2 In Chapter compares the investment motives of large shareholders in Japan and the United States. In the United States institutional investors, the leading players in the stock market, consistently pursue purely financial investments and have total freedom to buy and sell. Their relationship with the issuers of the stocks they own is temporary – they buy when they believe that the stock is undervalued and sell as soon as they consider it has become overvalued. Essentially they are third-party outsiders who make no commitment at all to the management. The risk they take is solely that stemming from price fluctuations in the market – not business risk. When such investment managers are dissatisfied with the management of a company, they typically sell off and walk away. This is in marked contrast to the behaviour of major corporate and institutional shareholders in Japan, whose main motivation to invest in stocks is, as explained later, to develop and strengthen their relationship with companies.

Part II

Japanese Capitalism

5 Japanese Economic and Financial Systems

5.1 STRATEGIC ALLOCATION OF RESOURCES

The Japanese economic and financial system that evolved after the Second World War can be regarded as the most successful example of a mixed economic system, as described in Chapter 1. Most people assume that Japan is a capitalist market economy based on the private ownership of a large part of its economic resources. Viewed as a resource allocation system, however, Japan can be regarded as somewhat closer to the elite-led, centrally planned economy than the US-type open-market economy. Indeed Japan is sometimes referred to as the most successful socialist economy.

Chalmers Johnson, who called Japan and other East Asian mixed economies with heavy government guidance and involvement 'developmental capitalist states', regarded the strategic allocation of economic resources to certain sectors, or targeting by the government, as the most conspicuous common feature of all the developmental capitalist economies.[1]

US capitalism has tried to resolve the problem of resource constraints by developing an open marketplace that attracts all necessary resources from all over the world. There they are traded by numerous participants and dispersed again domestically and internationally. Japan, on the other hand, has tried to allocate its scarce resources in such a way that the country can survive and prosper as a subsystem of the global market system.

In order to do this effectively, Japan has developed its own unique system of priority setting and resource allocation, including formal and informal networks of information sharing and consensus building, and interlocking, multiple, long-term relationships among financial and non-financial firms, all under strong governmental and bureaucratic guidance and close consultation between the government and the private sector.

Until recently, economic activities were broadly regulated, controlled and supervised by the government. The free market mechanism has also been used in Japan, but its role has been at best secondary in the resource allocation process and limited to areas not regarded as strategically important or to cases where there was no other alternative.

Managing this kind of system effectively and smoothly requires a well-designed and sophisticated infrastructure that is different from both the Soviet-type central planning and enforcement system and the US-type open market system.

An important part of this infrastructure are formal and informal network of politicians, bureaucrats and the business sector, which enable consensus to be reached and decisions to be made on the strategic allocation of resources, or targeting. Another part of the infrastructure are formal and informal social, economic, industrial and business systems, which implement the decisions made by the networks. The latter involves industry and business mobilising the public to promote the export-led industrial policies of MITI and other government agencies.

Table 1.1 listed some of the key features that are frequently pointed out as characteristic of postwar Japanese capitalism. Many of these features, which until recently have been accepted as desirable or necessary in Japan, widely violate, restrict, distort or reject the basic principles and rules of the free market system.[2]

The roles of the Japanese money and capital markets have also been very different from those found in the central marketplace. In the Japanese system, the primary role of the financial market has been to supply low-cost capital to nationally important industries and companies. The financial system, the policies and regulations for financial industries and institutions, the financial industry structure, the interest rate structure and monetary and capital market policies were designed and implemented in line with this objective. The low-interest-rate policy adopted until the 1970s provides the most overt evidence of Japan's financial policy. The unique share ownership structure, which enabled Japan to reduce the cost of equity capital, a major competitive weapon in Japan's push for exports, provides further evidence, although the full implication of the low cost of equity capital does not seem to have been clearly understood by the policy makers of Japan until today.

As shown in Table 5.1, the traditional Japanese financial system and capital market have also broadly violated, restricted, distorted or rejected the major principles and rules of an efficient, open and free capital market. Many of the traditional restrictions, regulations and guidelines on the financial system and capital market were gradually abolished during the 1980s through continuous internationalisation and deregulation. However, even today, some of the key elements of the traditional financial system, especially the main bank system and the unique share ownership structure, are still firmly in place.

With US capitalism it is assumed that, as a principle, the same price and other terms of trade are applied to all participants through an open, homogeneous market for numerous economic goods and services. All transactions should be completed on an 'on the spot' basis with 'arms-length' terms of trade, and a preferential long-term relationship is not expected to develop between or among the parties involved. In fact the US anti-trust laws strictly rule out special preferential arrangements and package deals between two parties or groups.

In the traditional Japanese system, the concept of an open, universal and homogeneous market has been neither developed nor accepted. Instead there are numerous closed or semi-closed submarkets in which special terms of trade are applied to reflect differences in the importance of the relationship between the parties involved. Unlike the homogeneous US market, to which everyone enjoys access on equal terms, the

TABLE 5.1 Characteristics of the traditional financial system

1. Isolation from the rest of the world	Foreign exchange control laws; foreign capital laws; severe restrictions on raising capital from overseas
2. High savings policy	Fiscal and institutional incentives for high savings; emphasis on bank deposits and postal savings; restraints on consumer credit and home mortgage loans; underdeveloped welfare programmes
3. Strategic allocation of capital	Allocation of capital in accordance with the priorities of industrial policies; strong emphasis on manufacturing and public utilities industries
4. Public financial institutions	Postal saving system supplementing and competing with private financial institutions; several government banks specialising in non-commercial loans and investments.
5. Capital allocation through banking system	Limited choice of financial products for small savers; underdeveloped money and bond market
6. Tight control of financial institutions	Channeling savings from household to industrial sector through a small number of financial institutions; strong control of the activities of financial institutions by the MOF and BOJ.
7. Interest rate controls	Adoption of low-interest-rate policy; tight controls on all interest rates and terms of new issues of bonds
8. Emphasis on collateral	Collateral required for all borrowing and bonds
9. Interlocking relationship between companies and financial institutions	Development of business group with the large banks at the centre; main bank system; stable and cross-ownership of stocks

Japanese market is an aggregation of numerous heterogeneous submarkets; some very closed, some semiclosed, some open. In Japanese capitalism it is accepted or taken for granted that different prices and other terms of trade can be applied to different parties depending on the relative importance of the relationship between the parties involved. Whereas US capitalism is based on the open market paradigm, Japanese capitalism is based much more on face-to-face negotiations between the parties involved.

In the sense that a major part of economic resource allocation has been based on the strategic or political judgment of the elite rather than going through an open market mechanism, the Japanese system can be characterised as somewhat closer to the centrally planned economy than to the US system. Japan is also closer to the centrally planned economy in that it has traditionally emphasised the equality of economic results, or economic equality, rather than the opportunity to participate, which is always identified with US capitalism. From the point of view of achieving economic equity among citizens, Japan has probably been the most successful of all major nations, including the former socialist economies. This is why Japan is sometimes lauded as the most successful socialist economy in the world.

One big difference between Japan and the centrally planned socialist economies, however, is that Japan has thrived in the international open market, while the latter tried to alienate themselves from it. As a result, as Japan's economic development efforts met with greater and greater success, economic and trade frictions grew with other nations in general and with the United States in particular. The Japanese system was designed and developed so that Japan, which was and is very poorly endowed with natural resources, lacked capital and basic technologies, and had a very small domestic market in the early years, could survive and prosper by taking advantage of the vast international marketplace with the United States at the centre.

As will be analysed in detail in the following chapters, Japan skillfully developed a unique and sophisticated system that accommodated the low profitability of large Japanese companies and helped them to survive, gain market share and grow in size in the international marketplace. Japan's success, however, was bound to create international friction.

5.2 THE INDIRECT FINANCING SYSTEM

The large discrepancy between the number of financial organisations in Japan and the United States, as shown in Table 5.2, is symbolic of the difference between the two systems. The extremely diversified format of the US system stands in marked contrast to the highly concentrated configuration of Japan's system.

Japan proved itself exceptional by carrying out postwar reconstruction and achieving high economic growth to become a major economic power without depending on foreign loans or capital to any significant degree. To accomplish these tasks,

TABLE 5.2 The number of major financial institutions in Japan and United States

Type of institution	*Japan*	*United States*
Commercial Banks	153	11 449
Life Insurance Companies	27	1944
Non-life Insurance Companies	25	3914
Securities Companies	210	7805
Investment Advisory Companies	615	18 000

Notes: The figures for Japan are for the end of calendar year 1991 for banks, securities companies and investment advisory companies, and for the end of fiscal year 1991 for life and non-life insurance companies. All US figures are for the end of calendar year 1992.

Sources: Japan: Nihon Ginko, *Economic Statistics Annual 1991* (Tokyo, 1992) for all groups except investment advisory companies, *1991 Fact Book*. (Tokyo Investment Advisory Industry Association of Japan 1992, for investment advisory companies.)
United States: FDIC Statistics on Banking (1994) for banks; American Council of Life Insurance, *1994 Life Insurance Fact Book*, for life insurance companies; Insurance Information Institute, *Property/Casualty Insurance Facts*, for non-life insurance companies; Securities and Exchange Commission (1995), *SEC Annual Report 1994*, for securities companies and investment advisory companies.

the Japanese leadership encouraged savings by the household sector and allocated these funds in accordance with the nation's priorities. This required the establishment of an 'indirect financing system', which relied on a limited number of large financial institutions (particularly large commercial banks) to act as intermediaries in the mobilisation and allocation of people's savings.[3]

A key condition for Japan's postwar economic development was the acquisition of foreign exchange. To carry out economic development in the face of scant indigenous raw materials, limited basic technologies and a scarcity of capital, domestic savings were not enough and large amounts of hard currency (dollars) were needed. Accordingly the expansion of exports became of urgent necessity, and strengthening the international competitiveness of Japan's major companies stood at the core of the nation's economic policy. To this end, Japanese companies adopted a common competitive strategy of marketing 'better and cheaper' (see Chapter 2) – a strategy that required Japanese companies to have steady access to low-cost capital regardless of their short-term financial performance.

Largely because Japan was small relative to the global economy, it was not necessary to assume that the cost of capital would be set by the open market and therefore uncontrollable. Rather a rational approach for Japan to survive in the international marketplace was to lower the cost of capital for 'strategically' important companies while rationing out the rest. Strategically important companies were typically involved in basic manufacturing, transportation, public utilities, and financial and international trade; were members of established *keiretsu* (business groups); had their stocks listed in the first section of the Tokyo and Osaka Stock Exchanges; had relationships with the main banks; enjoyed preferential treatment in public bond offerings; and a large proportion of their outstanding stocks were often stably and cross-held by 'relationship' investors.

Indeed Japan openly provided certain important industries with debt capital at artificially low interest rates for a long period of time.[4] Japan is not the only country to have done this in the interests of international competitiveness, but it has done so on an extensive scale and in a systematic way.

In *Strategic Capitalism* Calder emphasised the importance of the capital allocation mechanism in Japan,[5] and in particular the important role played by large commercial and industrial banks in this process. However, contrary to my argument, he paid little attention to the importance of equity capital, the share ownership structure and stock valuation in Japan's postwar economic development.

If one can develop a system that effectively reduces the cost of equity capital to below that prevailing in the open market, the result can be even more advantageous from a competitive standpoint. As will be discussed in detail in Part III, the unique features of Japan's financial and capital market – such as the main bank system, the practice of stable stockholding and the reciprocal cross-holding of stocks – have all made it possible for Japan's major companies to reduce substantially the cost of their equity capital. In contrast to the US system, a major feature of Japan's financial system has been the ability of large companies to procure relatively low-cost capital irrespective of their financial performance or profitability, as conventionally defined.

When designing a financial system that was able to provide a steady flow of capital on a priority basis to large companies at low cost, Japan adopted the following approach:

1. Financing industrial activities primarily through low-cost debt capital, and minimising the use of high-cost equity capital.
2. Increasing the use of debt while keeping the cost of capital low would have been difficult to achieve by raising debt and equity capital separately in an open market with a large number of outside investors. Accordingly a system was developed in which capital was provided primarily by a small number of financial institutions based on their long-term, interlocking relationship with the borrowing company, effectively offering a long-term commitment for both debt and equity capital as a package.

5.3 THE FINANCIAL POLICY OF LARGE JAPANESE COMPANIES

The full implications of the impact of Japan's traditional financial system on international competition will be elaborated in Part III. Here I would like to highlight its impact on the financial policy of large Japanese companies in contrast with that of US companies in the central marketplace. Tables 5.3 and 5.4 compare the key financial ratios of large companies in the industrial sectors of Japan and the United States since 1970 (book equity to total capital ratio, profit margins and return on shareholder's equity, or ROE). Compared with the United States, extensive use of financial leverage, or a very low equity ratio, and very low profitability stand out as major features of the financial policy of large Japanese companies.

If we look at the trend of the operating profit margin, a key profitability indicator, Japan started at the significantly low level of 5.4 per cent in 1970 and continued to deteriorate to just over 3 per cent in 1990. In contrast the United States remained surprisingly stable, fluctuating around 9 per cent over the two decades.

TABLE 5.3 Equity to total capital ratio of large Japanese and US companies

	Japan	*USA*
1970	21.5	53.8
1975	16.6	53.7
1980	20.9	49.6
1985	29.6	45.0
1990	36.4	40.2

Source: Comparative economic and financial statistics, Japan and other major countries (Tokyo, Bank of Japan, 1991)

TABLE 5.4 Trends in the profitability of large Japanese and US companies, 1971–94[1]

	Japan						United States				
	Gross margin (%)	Operating margin (%)	After tax margin (%)	ROE[2] (%)	EPS[3]	DPS[4]	Operating margin[5] (%)	After tax margin (%)	ROE[3] (%)	EPS[3]	DPS[4]
1971	13.9	5.4	2.1	14.8	8.4	3.5	10.0	5.0	10.8	6.0	3.2
1972	13.2	4.6	1.6	11.2	6.9	3.3	10.6	5.3	11.7	6.8	3.2
1973	13.3	4.8	1.7	11.9	8.0	3.3	11.7	6.0	14.2	8.9	3.5
1974	12.9	5.1	1.7	14.4	10.8	3.8	11.6	5.3	14.2	9.6	3.7
1975	11.6	4.2	1.1	10.0	8.1	3.8	10.4	4.6	12.1	8.6	3.7
1976	11.2	3.3	0.9	7.9	6.6	3.6	10.7	5.3	14.0	10.7	4.2
1977	11.7	3.8	1.1	9.7	8.7	3.9	10.6	5.1	13.9	11.5	5.0
1978	11.7	3.3	1.1	9.3	9.0	3.7	10.6	5.2	14.6	13.0	5.4
1979	12.4	3.6	1.3	9.9	10.4	3.8	10.7	5.6	16.5	16.3	5.9
1980	12.3	4.2	1.5	12.3	14.0	4.2	9.4	4.9	14.9	16.1	6.5
1981	11.6	3.9	1.4	11.7	14.6	4.4	8.9	4.9	14.4	16.7	7.0
1982	11.3	3.6	1.2	9.4	12.9	4.5	8.2	4.0	11.1	13.2	7.1
1983	11.0	3.2	1.2	8.9	13.5	4.5	9.0	4.4	12.1	14.8	7.3
1984	11.4	3.1	1.2	8.3	13.6	4.8	9.3	4.8	14.6	18.1	7.5
1985	11.7	3.4	1.3	9.0	16.1	5.1	8.8	3.8	12.1	15.3	7.9
1986	11.8	2.9	1.3	8.3	15.4	5.2	8.2	3.8	11.6	14.5	8.1
1987	12.0	2.4	1.2	6.0	11.9	5.0	9.0	4.7	15.1	20.3	8.7
1988	12.6	2.9	1.4	6.7	14.1	5.2	10.4	5.5	19.1	26.6	9.8
1989	13.5	3.5	1.6	7.9	18.5	5.8	10.2	5.0	18.5	26.8	12.0

TABLE 5.4 *(Continued)*

	Japan						*United States*				
	Gross margin (%)	*Operating margin (%)*	*After tax margin (%)*	*ROE*[2] *(%)*	*EPS*[3]	*DPS*[4]	*Operating margin*[5] *(%)*	*After tax margin (%)*	*ROE*[3] *(%)*	*EPS*[3]	*DPS*[4]
1990	12.5	3.3	1.7	8.1	21.6	6.3	9.5	4.2	16.2	24.8	12.7
1991	13.0	3.3	1.8	7.7	23.0	6.6	8.1	2.9	10.8	16.9	12.5
1992	13.1	2.8	1.5	6.0	18.9	6.7	8.1	3.2	13.4	19.1	13.0
1993	12.9	2.2	1.0	3.7	12.2	6.5	8.9	3.6	16.0	21.9	12.5
1994	na	2.0	0.9	2.8	9.1	5.7	9.9	5.2	21.9	33.1	13.0

Notes:
1. Year ending March for Japan; year ending December for the United States. Figures for Japan are averages for NRI 350 companies obtained from NRI 400 series compiled by the Nomura Research Institute. Figures for the United States are averages for the companies in the S&P industrial composite stock index compiled by the Standard and Poor Corporation.
2. ROE = return on equity.
3. EPS = earning per share.
4. DPS = dividend per share.
5. After depreciation charges.

Sources: Japan: Nomura Research Institute (1995), NRI 400 Handbook, Tokyo. United States: Standard and Poor Corporation (1995), Standard and Poor Analyst's Handbook, New York.
NRI 400 Handbook (Tokyo, Nomura Research Institute 1995) In Japan; Standard and Poor Analyst's Handbook (New York, Standard and Poor 1995)

For return on equity (ROE) there was an even more dramatic long-term downward trend in Japan. The United States, in contrast, showed much greater stability with a slight upward trend. It looks as though Japan's ROE was as high or sometimes even higher than that of the United States in the earlier years, but this was not really the case because the equity base for Japanese companies was very small compared with that of the United States. If we are to take the average historical ROE as a proxy with which to estimate the required return on equity, we must also take into consideration how much financial risk was involved.

In the central marketplace, all companies have to maintain a fairly large equity cushion in order to raise debt capital at reasonable terms. Although there has been a tendency to use somewhat more debt capital than before in recent years in the United States, the long-term average debt to equity ratio for a well-managed US company is thought to be something like one to one. In the central marketplace the kind of low equity ratio that Japanese companies enjoyed in the earlier years would be inconceivable, and even if it were possible the required ROE would have been much higher than reported by Japanese companies. Thus, if we take into consideration the very low equity ratio, Japanese ROE in those earlier years was much lower than that for US companies.

In the central marketplace, a low equity ratio and low profitability are clear evidence of the weakness of a company. A company with such financial characteristics will be given a low price – earnings ratio and a low bond rating, and will be handicapped in raising both debt and equity capital as well as other necessary resources, and thus will lose out in the competition for market share.

However, if a local system tolerates or even encourages such financial characteristics and continues to provide capital and other resources, these characteristics will not constitute weakness but will become a major source of strength in the competition for survival and growth in the open marketplace, which welcomes better and cheaper goods. Indeed this is what the Japanese system provided to the large Japanese companies that played a key role as dollar earners in the international market for exported manufactured goods.

The analysis of the flow of funds in the United States, and Japan also reflects the very different approaches of these two countries in their capital allocation patterns in the non-financial sector. Figure 5.1 compares the capital-raising patterns of the non-financial sector – that is, business, government and household – through the broadly defined market for debt capital in the two nations.[6] Here borrowing is divided into four categories: (1) borrowing indirectly through financial intermediaries, (2) borrowing from financial intermediaries through the open market, (3) borrowing by offering debt securities in the open market and (4) direct borrowing without any financial intermediation or by offering securities in the open market.

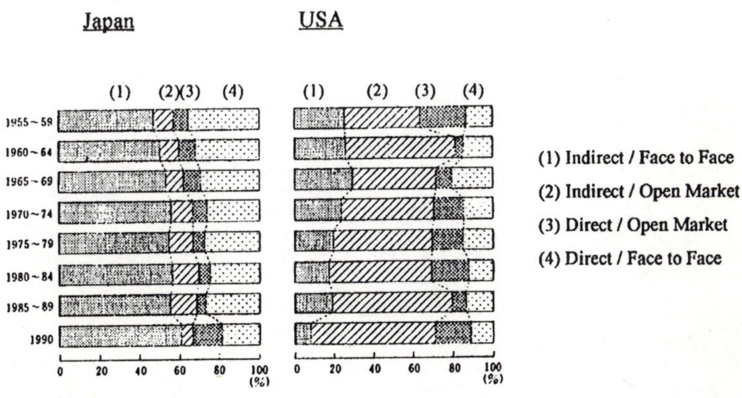

Source: Economic White Paper for Fiscal Year 1993 (Tokyo, Economic Planning Agency, 1993).

FIGURE 5.1 Comparison of the flow of funds to the non-financial sector, Japan and the United States

Traditionally, the concept of indirect financing has characterised the dependence of large Japanese companies on financial intermediaries, especially large commercial banks (main banks), for their capital requirements. The term indirect financing has been used to contrast the Japanese approach to the 'direct' financing of the US system, which means raising capital by issuing securities through the open market.

However if we emphasise the importance of resource allocation through face-to-face negotiations between the parties involved as the essence of the traditional Japanese system, and if we contrast it with the US approach of allocating resources through a homogeneous, open market, the distinction between borrowing through a face-to-face deal and through the open market seems to be more relevant and fundamental. If we look at Figure 5.1 from this point of view, we can conclude that the US system has always allocated capital primarily through the open market and Japan has always relied heavily on face-to-face deals. This conclusion can be extended to the allocation of equity capital, as will be discussed in the following chapter.

6 The Unique Features of the Japanese Stock and Share Ownership Structure

6.1 THE UNIQUE SHARE OWNERSHIP STRUCTURE

As long as value-creation activities are mostly entrusted to investor-owned companies, all nations – the United States and Japan included – will face the challenge of reducing the cost of equity capital to a reasonable level. US capitalism has tried to achieve this goal by requiring public disclosure of information and developing a large number of investment professionals. In contrast the policy in Japan has been geared to constructing long-standing, interlocking relationships among companies and between companies and major financial institutions, and practices such as stable shareholding and the reciprocal cross-holding of stocks constitute an essential part of this. The share ownership structure in Japan and the United States clearly reflect the differences in these approaches.

Table 6.1 shows the result of a survey conducted by the Japanese Ministry of International Trade and Industry (MITI) concerning the top five shareholders of major Japanese and US companies.[1] As can been seen from the table, the major shareholders in the United States are largely represented by 'pure' financial investors – that is, both institutions and individuals investing purely for financial returns. In Japan ownership is overwhelmingly weighted towards so-called relationship share-

TABLE 6.1 Comparison of the stock ownership structure in Japan and the United States (composition of the top five shareholders' per cent)

	Japan	*US*
Institutional investors	15	44
Relationship investors:		
Financial institutions	47	12
Other companies	11	9
Parent and group companies	17	2
Founders and families	4	10
Individuals	3	19
Others	4	4
Total	100	100

Source: Ministry of International Trade and Industry (ed.) *Comparison of the Behaviour of Japanese and US Firms* (Tokyo: MITI, 1989), pp. 100–1.

holders, where investment goes hand in hand with a key business relationship such as between a parent company and its subsidiaries, a bank and its borrowers, a company and a major customer, or between companies within the same business group.

In short, a major difference in the share ownership structure between the United States and Japan is the preponderance of 'pure' financial investors in the former versus the preponderance of investors with relationship motives in the latter. Indeed the very concept of stable shareholders in Japan amounts to a company selecting its major shareholders, and this clearly contravenes the basic spirit of companies going public in the US system, in which stocks are widely available to general investors. However Japan's approach – whereby resource allocation and the terms of trade are mutually decided through face-to-face negotiations between the parties concerned – can be considered highly rational and consistent with the country's economic system.

Another major difference between the shareholding patterns of Japan and the United States is the extent of cross-holding. Cross-holding occurs when two firms hold each other's shares, either directly, as when firm A holds shares in firm B and B holds shares in A, or indirectly, as when A holds shares in B, B holds shares in C, and C holds shares in A. Although there are no official statistics on cross-holding *per se* (as opposed to shareholding), the cross-holding of stocks among listed companies and banks is widespread in Japan. According to a recent Fair Trade Commission report on the six major corporate groups, for example, cross-ownership arrangements existed in 76 per cent of the member companies of the Mitsui, Mitsubishi and Sumitomo groups at the end of fiscal year 1992. Twenty eight per cent of the outstanding stocks of these companies were cross-held among group members.[2]

In contrast, cross-holdings, which may unfavourably affect financial results, are hardly conceivable in the United States, where the managers are evaluated primarily in terms of financial results such as ROE. Cross-holding tends to overstate the equity base and if it results in accommodating low-profitability management, as this paper argues, it will bring about a low reported ROE. Moreover if cross-holding relationships result in reciprocal or preferential business dealings, as is often claimed in Japan, they may be seen as contravening US antitrust laws. One may therefore conclude that the cross-holding of stocks in the Japanese sense will be marginal or non-existant in the United States.

A third difference in the share ownership structure involves the relationship between issuers and banks and other financial institutions. In recent years in both the United States and Japan, large companies have substantially diversified their sources of financing, particularly in the area of debt and hybrid securities that possess both debt and equity characteristics. For example junk bonds in the United States and convertibles and bonds with warrant in Japan have come into wide use.

A significant difference between Japanese and US companies is the way in which they diversify their sources of capital.

In the United States, companies have diversified not only in the type of financing used but also in their relationships with creditors and investors, who may have conflicting or competing interests. Companies are creating all kinds of financial claims with differing risk/return characteristics to maximise the market value of the cash flow generated by the business, and selling these to investors who are only interested in one particular 'slice' of the total corporate cash flow (see Chapter 3). These securities essentially represent bundles of contracts that stipulate the conditions and relative seniority of each against the total cash flow. Although this poses no problem when the business is going well, the conflict of interests between creditors and investors can lead to a scramble for a portion of the diminished cash flow once the business turns sour.

In the Japanese case, although major companies have gradually distanced themselves from their banks in recent years, the traditional pattern has been for a small number of large financial institutions to commit themselves, virtually as a package, to the company at all levels of its capital structure. The most notable example is the case of a relationship with a main bank, in which a company establishes a particularly close relationship with a large commercial and industrial bank that serves not only as the main supplier of short- and long-term loans and the major holder of straight and convertible bonds, but also as one of the major shareholders. This stands in sharp contrast with the US system, where banking laws prohibit commercial banks from owning stocks. This kind of relationship is maintained, though to a lesser degree, in almost all the major Japanese financial institutions dealings with corporate clients. These institutions include long-term credit banks, trust banks and life insurance companies. As a result, the diversification of financing for most large Japanese companies thus far has meant a diversification of forms of financing, but not a diversification of relationships with creditors and investors.

When a financial institution commits itself to all the capital needs of a company, conflicts of interests among those laying claim to different slices of the total corporate cash flow become much less acute. Both company managers and financial institutions can focus on the growth of the business, but at the cost of a relatively low return on equity capital. Moreover this arrangement allows companies to raise debt capital with a low interest charge coverage and a high debt to equity ratio.

6.2 THE CHARACTERISTICS OF RELATIONSHIP INVESTMENT

Stock investment based on relationships results in a considerably different stock market from the one that results when pure financial investment is the norm. I call the Japanese approach 'relationship investment'. Table 6.2 summarises the main differences between the US and Japanese approaches.

In the US approach, the primary purpose of stock investment is to realise the highest possible financial return. In contrast, in the Japanese approach major shareholders have multiple purposes. Although making a financial gain via dividends and capital gains is one of the motives, it is not usually the sole or even necessarily the main purpose. Rather, shareholding in Japan represents an important device to cement business relationships between two companies or between a company and a financial institution. Banks holds shares, but they also lend large amounts, hold bonds, manage settlement accounts and provide a range of financial services. Insurance companies are principal shareholders, but like banks they provide loans and hold bonds, and sell insurance products to the firm, its affiliated companies and employees. Manufacturing and trading companies hold shares in the firms that they sell to or purchase from. Cross-holding also serves to guarantee mutual trust, and cooperation among the management of companies and financial institutions helps protect them against the threat of takeover.[3]

Such relationships offer an obvious competitive advantage in terms of the cost of capital. If the main purpose of stock

TABLE 6.2 Comparison of the nature of major shareholders in Japan and the United States

	Japan	*United States*
Investment objectives	Multiple: financial, relationship, insurance etc.	Pure financial (dividend plus capital gain)
Degree of freedom to sell	Small	Large
Relationship with the issuing company	Long-term, interlocking, de facto business partner, de facto insider	Temporary, buy if underpriced, sell if overpriced, arm's-length outsider
Type of risk involved	Business and financial market risks	Pure financial market risk
Means of controlling risks	Sharing information, strong commitment to the management, developing interlocking relations	Disclosure, fundamental analysis, diversification

investment is to develop and maintain a long-term and interlocking relationship, and if the major shareholders' total return includes non-financial returns from other parts of the relationship they can easily tolerate a relatively low return on their equity investment.

Even more important is the day-to-day sharing of business information that goes on between a company and a financial institution. Because of the long-term, comprehensive relationship that is fostered, information is shared at all organisational levels through formal and informal contacts. This aspect is especially important in a company's relationship with its main bank. Main banks not only bear the credit and investment risks of their major clients, but they also essentially share the business risks as well, and are thus for all practical purposes a business partner of the client company. In its role as a business partner, the main bank naturally commits itself to providing all types of capital, and in return it expects full access to information about the company; if necessary it will even post its own managers to the company.[4] Such involvement effectively reduces the risk borne by the main bank and therefore lowers the cost of capital, or the minimum required financial return, for the company.

In the US approach, whereby companies have a broad base of creditors and investors, each with its own self-interest, the oft-cited problem of agency costs may become a serious issue. Agency costs are costs that arise from the imperfect monitoring of managers by investors and conflicts of interests among different classes of investor. The Japanese approach could well be effective in reducing these agency costs. Bank–company relationships similar to those in Japan can also be found in Germany, France and elsewhere, but the idea of long-term, interlocking relationships runs counter to the philosophy of the US system, which is based on the belief that companies, banks and investors should remain at arms' length.[5]

One of the conditions for efficient stock price formation is an emphasis on pure financial returns rather than the control aspect of common stock investment. In Japanese relationship investment, however, the control aspect of common stock investment is given much more importance.

It should be noted that in Japan economic activities are, in large part, carried out by companies that are investor-owned with shares traded on the stock exchange, and are run by professional managers. In this sense corporate ownership and management are as fully separated in Japan as in the United States. However, since three fourths of all outstanding shares of listed companies are held by business partners or financial institutions with whom the company has close business relations, ownership and management can be said to be unified in Japan in a unique way. Yet unlike entrepreneur-owned companies where ownership and management is typically unified, the top managers of large Japanese companies and banks representing corporate shareholders almost always consist of hired managers working on a salaried basis who do not themselves invest a large amount of their own money in the company or bear much personal risk as owners. For this reason, relationship shareholders can easily sacrifice financial returns on equity investment, if other goals such as expanding the business, increasing exports or maintaining life-long employment are of higher priority.

6.3 BANK ASSET LIABILITY MANAGEMENT AND RELATIONSHIP INVESTMENT

A fundamental dilemma in the traditional financial system of Japan is that large commercial banks whose primary source of capital consists of short-term fixed-interest-rate deposits, capital that represents the lowest return and the lowest risk, are also required to be major suppliers of equity capital, the riskiest part of the corporate capital structure. For the commercial banks, holding a large portfolio of common stocks can be very risky because of the mismatch between the degree of risk in their assets and liabilities.

Any commercial bank in the pure open market economy faces a certain degree of interest-rate risk arising from fluctuating market interest rates combined with some mismatch between the average maturity of its deposits on the one hand and loans and investment on the other. In addition it is exposed to the risk of bad loans and non-performing loans (default risk). A certain amount of bank equity is needed as a cushion to absorb these two types of risk, which are inherent in commercial banking operations. The recent effort by the Bank for International Settlements (BIS) to introduce a minimum bank equity ratio reflects the harmonisation of the rules governing this safety cushion for the banks of all member nations.

The traditional Japanese banking system is not based on the logic of the open market system. On the contrary the Japanese system has been tightly controlled and regulated for an effective allocation of capital to areas of high priority without being bothered by the ever-fluctuating and uncontrollable marketplace. Accordingly the interest rates paid on bank deposits (or the cost of deposits) and standard commercial and industrial lending rates (or return on assets) have been strictly pegged to the official discount rate set by the Bank of Japan. This system has protected banks from interest-rate risk, and no matter what happened to the money and credit market, commercial banks have been able to secure a stable spread between lending and borrowing rates. Also, by establishing a strong consensus within the system that no major companies should go bankrupt, banks have been protected from a default risk. Since minor defaults and bad loans have been well taken care of through reserves for bad debts, the large commercial banks really have not needed a significant cushion against lending risk, unlike their counterparts in the United States. As a result, the average book equity ratio of the major Japanese banks has been significantly lower than that of US banks. Also, they have been able to use their equity capital as a permanent source of funds for their relationship investment in the common stocks of major client companies.

Until the mid 1980 the practice was to restrict the size of relationship equity investment within the bank equity capital on the book. Management of the relationship equity portfolio had been outside the narrow banking operation, and rather than seeking to maximise the total return on the investment, cash-flow matching was the primary concern so that banks could meet their stable dividend commitment out of their dividend receipts from their equity portfolios. Since their equity investment was valued at lower of either the historic average cost of investment or current market value of the portfolio by bank examiners (Ministry of Finance and Bank of Japan), bankers naturally desired a stock market that priced stocks substantially higher than their average book cost.

6.4 HIGH VALUATION OF LOW-PROFITABILITY, LOW-GROWTH COMPANIES

How then did the Japanese stock market contribute to the 'better and cheaper' strategy of Japan in its role as the supreme court of the economic value-creation process? In this and the following chapters we will look into this issue in detail.

The PER model introduced in Chapter 3 is a useful tool with which to compare the nature of different stock markets. The model presented in the simplified form of: PER = (expected dividend payout ratio)/(investors' expected return from investing in the stock (*r*) – expected growth rate of dividend per share (*g*)) – tells us the following. If other factors are held equal, (1) the higher the dividend payout ratio, (2) the higher the expected growth rate and (3) the lower the expected return of investors, the higher stock price, or PER. Of the three determinants of PER in this model, the first two represent fundamental company factors and the third, investor factor.

Under US capitalism the stock market is expected to encourage companies that produce a high return on their shareholders' capital, or high ROE, by giving them a high valuation, or high PER, and discourage low ROE companies by giving them a low valuation. As can be seen in Table 6.3, this is not the case with Japanese capitalism. Japan is unique among the major industrialized economies in that it gives an extremely high valuation (PER) for the least profitable companies. In other words, the Japanese stock market highly values companies with low profitability and hence low growth per share.

Based on the US and Japanese financial data in Table 5.4, let us first compare company factors in the United States and Japan. Japan's average dividend payout ratio was considerably lower than that of the United States during the 1970s and 1980s. Large Japanese industrial companies paid out roughly 30 per cent of their after-tax earnings as a cash dividend, whereas their US counterparts paid out roughly 50 per cent. The dividend payout factor tells us that the US PER should be higher if other things are equal.

Next let us compare the growth factor. Since what matters is the growth rate of one stake of ownership in a company, the relevant fundamental parameter that determines growth is ROE, or the average productivity of equity capital. With the constant growth model, growth is shown by the portion of the increase in ownership that is retained (not paid out as dividends) and reinvested for future growth. Thus the expected growth rate is estimated by expected ROE × (1 − payout ratio). A comparison of the ROE and dividend payment ratios for the United States and Japan suggests that the expected

TABLE 6.3 International comparison of corporate profitability and PER

	Number of companies	*Net after-tax margin (%)*	*Return on equity (%)*	*PER (times)*
Britain	94	7.1	20.2	14
France	40	5.9	15.5	17
Germany	39	2.4	13.7	27
Japan	309	2.4	8.6	60
US	359	5.6	19.1	22

Source: 'The Global 1000', *Business Week*, 15 July 1991.

growth factor should be significantly higher in the United States. In fact the realised average annual growth rates of EPS (earnings per share) and DPS (dividends per share) have been significantly higher in the United States, and thus, other factors being equal, the US PER should be significantly higher than that for Japan.

If all company factors are taken together, the US fundamental factors were much more favourable for stock prices than those in Japan during the 1970s and 1980s. Therefore the only logical explanation for the big difference in PER in favour of Japan lies in the uniqueness of Japan's investor factors, in particular that companies with a very poor financial performance are highly valued. In fact, if we estimate the investors' expected return, which was consistent with average PER and company factors during the 1980s for Japan and the United States, we would get something like 5.7 per cent for Japan and 11.9 per cent for the United States (Table 6.4). While the US figure reflects a 3–4 per cent risk premium on top of the risk-free, short-term interest rate, the Japanese figure seems to bear little or no risk premium over the short-term interest rate. The low expected return, and especially the very small risk premium associated with investment in stocks, lies at the heart of the unique Japanese method of valuation in the stock market.

TABLE 6.4 Estimated expected return for investors, Japan and the United States

	Japan	*USA*
PER (Price-earnings-ratio)	40	15
Payout ratio (5-year average, %)	33	45
ROE (5-year average, %)	7.3	16.1
Internal growth rate (5-year average, %)	4.9	8.9
Expected return (%)	5.7	11.9

6.5 UNIQUE FEATURES OF COMMON STOCK IN JAPAN

As described in Chapter 4, the majority of common stock investors in the central marketplace are financially oriented outsiders who have an arms-length relationship with borrowing companies. There, the ideal market is one that promptly and properly reflects investors' collective expectations about companies' ability to generate cash flows. In the Japanese market, on the other hand, stock prices are not valued efficiently in the US sense as more than two thirds of the shares of public companies are held stably, and a large proportion of them are cross-held among friendly corporate shareholders based on interlocking and long-term business relationships. Japan's relationship investment represents a third approach to stock investment, which can be distinguished from both the castle in the air approach and the fundamental approach described in Chapter 4. It is different from the other two approaches in many aspects, including the fact that stocks are held not for financial return but as a means of developing, strengthening and maintaining long-term and interlocking relationships between or among broadly defined corporate business partners.

As long as the business relationships continue, the shares are held stably and are seldom sold for financial gain. Thus a large proportion of stocks are illiquid. In addition most companies commit themselves to fixed cash dividend payments, typically five to 10 yen per share, as long as they are profitable, as if the stocks were quasi-fixed-income securities or preferred stocks. Also, it was traditional that virtually all new equity issues were made at par (50 yen in most cases) and placed with existing shareholders on a preemptive right basis. The practice of stable shareholding combined with a fixed and stable dividend commitment and par value preemptive issues effectively changed the nature of the Japanese stocks from pure common stocks to something like preferred stocks with a unique option feature. It should be noted that stocks with added features that limit downside risk should be valued not as a pure common stock but as a hybrid or synthetic security possessing characteristics of fixed-income securities with some kind of option. By defining Japanese stocks as quasi-fixed-income securities with unique option features, we can cast some new light on the unique behaviour of the Japanese stock market.

6.6 CHANGING PATTERNS OF NEW EQUITY ISSUES

Before analysing stock valuation in Japan, let me first draw attention to the shift in the pattern of new common equity issues over time (Table 6.5). The post-war period can be divided into two phases based on the nature of new equity issues. Until about the middle of the 1970s almost all new equity issues were offered at par value to existing shareholders on a preemptive right basis, and often a small number of 'free distribution' shares were combined with new issues. For example, in the case of one-to-one new equity issue with additional 0.1 free distribution (one free share given to every ten shares), the holders of one share were entitled to an additional share at the cost of 45 yen regardless of the market price at the time of the new issue. Stock prices largely reflected the fixed cash dividend streams as though they were fixed income obligations infinite without maturity, combined with option values of the preemptive rights for new issues.

This system was challenged during the 1970s when new companies in the emerging industries started to issue stocks at market prices based on expected future cash-flow growth per share. These new stocks were closer to pure common stocks in the US sense as they bore full residual risk and had no stable shareholders or main banks behind them, representing for the first time the high-risk, high-return segment in the Japanese capital market. The concept of PER was also introduced, along with the idea of new issues at market prices. Companies that made new public offerings at market prices typically commanded significantly higher stock prices than existing companies whose stocks were primarily valued according to

TABLE 6.5 Changing pattern of new equity issues (all listed companies)

	Total new equity financing		*Pattern of new issues*		
	No. of companies	*Billion yen*	*Right offering at par value (%)*	*Public offering at current market price (%)*	*Others (%)*
1960	419	447.5	88.7	11.2	0.1
1961	644	671.6	90.2	9.6	0.2
1962	590	543:0	96.3	3.6	0.1
1963	536	444.5	96.2	2.2	1.6
1964	421	447.5	98.9	0.4	0.7
1965	101	142.9	98.2	0.1	1.7
1966	224	193.9	93.9	1.2	4.9
1967	234	252.8	95.7	3.0	1.3
1968	230	324.1	95.0	3.6	1.4
1969	390	529.7	87.8	11.2	1.0
1970	375	661.3	80.0	19.1	0.9
1971	252	541.1	71.8	18.3	0.9
1972	429	1298.2	26.6	66.3	7.1
1973	316	731.4	41.3	53.6	5.1
1974	323	612.6	58.3	40.7	1.0
1975	219	902.4	72.0	27.0	1.0
1976	284	823.4	34.0	64.7	1.3

TABLE 6.5 *(Continued)*

	Total new equity financing		*Pattern of new issues*		
	No. of companies	*Billion yen*	*Right offering at par value (%)*	*Public offering at current market price (%)*	*Others (%)*
1977	330	709.4	30.2	65.7	4.1
1978	250	1032.9	29.8	64.1	6.1
1979	253	660.5	19.4	70.3	10.3
1980	256	1160.1	15.2	78.1	6.7
1981	285	1793.2	26.8	71.4	1.8
1982	172	1015.4	18.3	79.3	2.4
1983	126	849.5	16.7	65.5	17.8
1984	153	814.8	8.5	87.2	4.3
1985	131	651.3	28.6	67.2	4.2
1986	110	631.7	19.0	75.1	5.9
1987	149	2083.9	22.9	71.7	5.4
1988	236	4563.8	21.8	76.0	2.2
1989	326	7560.0	13.7	82.8	3.5
1990	98	664.6	42.0	29.7	28.3
1991	60	342.7	61.5	9.7	28.8
1992	34	151.7	37.7	5.4	56.9

Source: Zoshi Hakusho (White Paper on New Equity Financing), Tokyo, Junkan Shoji Homu, 1993 no. 1325

companies whose stocks were primarily valued according to the fixed income factor.

Because of the success of this new equity issue method, many large established companies naturally followed suit, and since about 1980 virtually all new equity issues have been made at or near the current market prices.

Due to this shift in the pattern of new issues, coupled with the shift in the valuation of stocks, I will analyse stock price behaviour in two phases:

(1) the early years when new equity issues were made at par, and
(2) the period since new issues came to be offered at the market price.

Table 6.6 shows how the two segments of the stock market shifted from the first phase to the second in terms of average price zones. Before 1970, when almost all new equity issues were made at par, the majority of stocks were priced below 300 yen, largely reflecting their fixed income values arising from stable fixed dividends. This feature was most visible during the 1950s. During the 1970s, when emerging companies started to offer new issues at market prices that were 10 times or more higher than par values, based on growth expectations, the segment with high stock prices (500 yen or higher in the table) began to grow. Around 1980 more than half of all listed stocks were priced above 500 yen. During the 1980s, when virtually all new equity issues were made at market prices, the valuation of stocks shifted to a method based on growth expectation, and almost all stocks were priced above 1000 yen. The ever rising trend of the average PER for the entire Japanese market should be seen as the gradual and long-term shift from phase one to phase two.

TABLE 6.6 Shift in the average stock price (% of companies in each price zone)

	Stock price						
	Below 100 yen	*101 – 300 yen*	*301 – 500 yen*	*501 – 1000 yen*	*1001 – 2000 yen*	*Above 2000 yen*	*Average (yen)*
1950	88	11	–	–	–	–	74.00
1955	65	34	–	–	–	–	108.17
1960	30	57	9	4	–	–	167.54
1965	59	38	3	–	–	–	99.56
1970	45	47	6	2	–	–	181.58
1975	17	61	15	6	–	–	268.95
1980	2	39	30	15	3	1	382.92
1985	–	15	33	33	11	7	682.47
1986	–	10	17	36	17	10	866.18
1987	–	2	17	45	24	12	1103.85
1988	–	–	3	46	34	16	1294.17
1989	–	–	–	13	58	30	1579.99
1990	–	–	8	44	31	17	1577.50

Note: The total may not be 100 due to rounding.

Source: Developed from Tokyo Stock Exchange statistics.

7 Stock Valuation in Japan: Phase One

7.1 COMMITMENT TO A STABLE, FIXED DIVIDEND

The concept of offering existing shareholders new equity issues at par value on a preemptive basis is now outdated, but at the time it was very consistent with the traditional relationship-based Japanese financial system, with the main banks at the centre. Understanding the nature of this concept is nonetheless very useful and relevant to understanding the behaviour of Japanese investors and the stock market today. Therefore I would like to review in detail the basic logic of the old system and how it functioned.

The strong commitment to maintaining fixed dividends per share at any cost was considered very important in the old system. Maintaining a dividend of five yen or 10 per cent of the par value was considered to be the minimum requirement for the management of any respectable, established public company. Since dividends were in principle paid out of reported current earnings, companies should and did cut or skip dividends when their earnings dropped or ran into deficit. However cutting or skipping dividends was regarded as a major breach of a company's commitment to its stable shareholders, akin to defaulting on the periodic repayment of debt or bank borrowings. As a result, if the earnings drop was considered temporary, many companies tried to maintain dividends by creating extraordinary gains.

The expected dividend per share was five yen for most major companies, including banks, electricity and gas companies, railroad companies and many established manufacturing and trading companies. Other companies paid somewhat higher dividends, but high profitability was socially unacceptable and therefore high dividends were discouraged. As a result, companies paying dividends of 10 yen or more were somewhat rare.

The uniformity of the dividend policy among Japanese companies remains until today. Figure 7.1, which shows the distribution of dividends per share for all companies listed on the first section of the Tokyo Stock Exchange, tells us how stable this practice has been. In the year ending March 1971, when new issues at par was a firm rule, the average dividend per share for all companies was 8.1 yen, with a standard deviation of 11.07 per cent. Most companies paid dividends of between zero and 10 yen. In the year ending March 1994, well after the practice of new issues at market price had been firmly established, the average dividend was 7.6 yen, somewhat lower than in 1971, partly because of the larger number of companies without any dividend, and the standard deviation was 7.88 per cent, even smaller than that for 1971. And still most companies were paying dividends of between zero and 12 yen. In other words the fixed-income nature of Japanese stock did not change at all during those years. If you compare this distribution with that of the S & P 500, the majority of Japanese companies fall under 10 cents below the extreme low end in the US diagram.

The most important condition for an additional issue of equity was that the current dividend per share would continue after the additional shares had been issued. Unless the after-tax income would be sufficiently greater than that required to maintain the current dividend, the additional issue of equity was impossible. Therefore one of the most watched-for financial ratios in those days was after-tax income as a percentage of average paid-in capital (the par value portion of the shareholders' equity section on the balance sheet). If this ratio increased to 15–20 per cent for a company paying a five yen or 10 per cent of par dividend, the market started to expect another round of equity issue and the share price started to reflect the value of the preemptive right of existing stock holders to purchase new issues at par value.

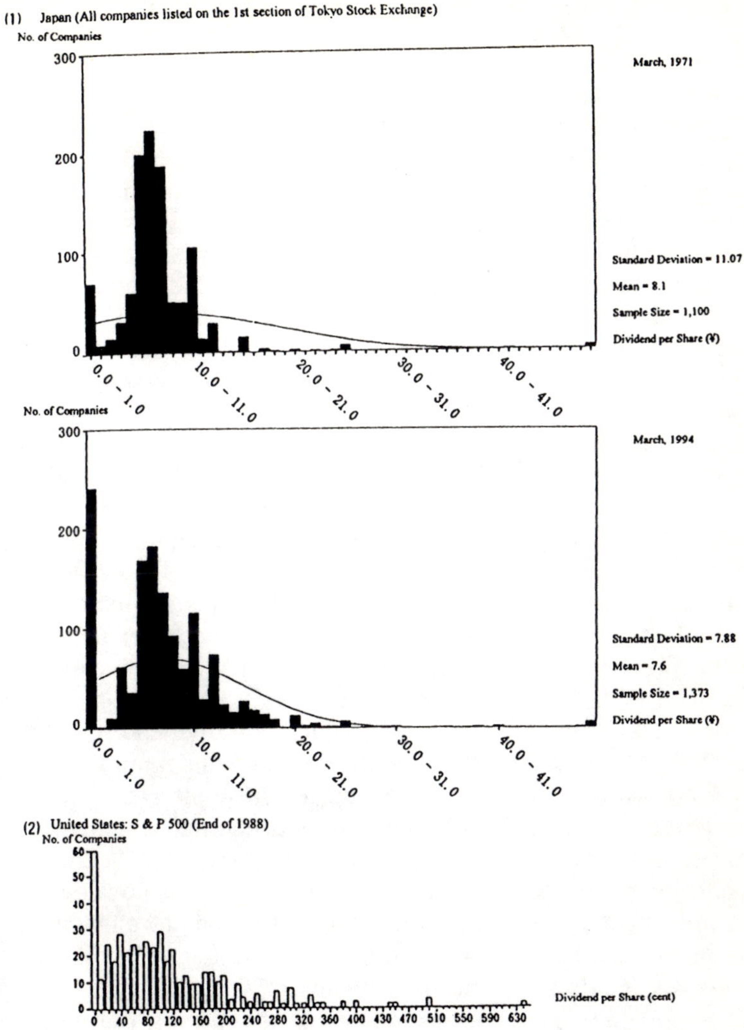

Source: Original data were obtained from Standard & Poor's; for the USA and from Nomura Research Institute in Japan.

FIGURE 7.1 US–Japan comparison of the distribution of dividends per share

7.2 THE LOGIC OF STOCK VALUATION DURING PHASE ONE

It was not a mere coincidence that the average stock prices of major companies during the 1950s and 1960s were less than one fourth to one fifth of those that prevailed during the 1980s. Common stocks in those days were valued as if they were fixed-income securities based on stable dividend flows plus a premium for the preemptive right to future new issues at par.

How did five yen, or 10 per cent of par value, come to be the minimum expected level of dividends? This was largely due to the fact that the main banks and other financial institutions, including trust banks and life insurance companies, with fixed-interest-type liabilities were the major stable shareholders. From the point of view of these institutions, holding a large amount of common stocks, the riskiest of all financial assets, was suicidal. There was therefore, a strong desire among them to turn common stocks into some kind of quasi-fixed-income securities by demanding that borrowing companies commit themselves to stable dividend payments. Since the interest rates charged by major banks and other lending institutions were held at approximately 10 per cent on average during the 1950s and 1960s, it was only natural that they should ask companies to pay the equivalent dividend rate per par value, or five yen per share. In those day the main portion of the portfolios of trust banks and life insurance companies constituted, like those of banks, direct lending to industrial and commercial companies at long-term prime rates. Securing a current return similar to a lending portfolio was considered an important precondition for these institutions to engage in stable relationship shareholding. For these financial institutions dividends were the only means of securing a periodic return on their stock investments for accounting purposes, because as stable shareholders they were not expected to realise capital gains by selling stocks in the market. The cost of investment was always at par value or less in their books.

For large commercial banks, the need to earn a return on their common stock portfolios was not as crucial as for trust banks and life insurance companies. Nevertheless for main banks too the 10 per cent stable dividend on 50 yen, the book cost of their relationship investment in stocks, was a very desirable one. For these stable shareholders, what was the theoretical value of an investment that delivered a stable five-yen cash dividend per annum in perpetuity? Using a 10 per cent interest charge as the opportunity cost of investment, this value was 50 yen, or five yen divided by 0.1. This was the reason why 50 yen was considered a fair price for any new issues of equity for these stable shareholders. In this manner the idea of new equity issue at par was closely linked to companies' five yen, or 10 per cent of par, dividend commitment.

Of course this investment vehicle had a value of more than 50 yen for those investors whose opportunity cost of investment was less than 10 per cent. In fact small outsider investors for the main players in the secondary market, the opportunity cost of investment was significantly lower than 10 per cent. For example the annual interest rate on bank deposits was set at 5–6 per cent in normal times during the 1950s and 1960s. If we use, for simplicity, 5 per cent as the average opportunity cost, or discount rate, for small investors in those days, a financial asset that delivered a five-yen cash dividend in perpetuity would be worth 100 yen rather than 50 yen. For those investors with only bank deposits or postoffice savings as a realistic alternative, a common stock with high liquidity, a stable cash dividend and a main-bank relationship to back it was an attractive investment opportunity with a limited downside risk.

Now, what is the value of the preemptive right to subscribe to any future equity issue at par for those outsider investors with a 5 per cent opportunity cost? Suppose a company were to issue one additional share for each existing share and also commit to maintain a five-yen dividend after the new issue. Since the expected cash flow per share before and after the new issue would not change, the theoretical value of the stock would remain at 100 yen before and after the new issue. Since the holders of existing stock have the right to purchase at 50 yen a new share with a theoretical value of 100 yen, the right would have a market price, or premium, of 50 yen before the right expires. Thus the day before the right expires, the theoretical market price of the existing stock would close at 150 yen – 100 yen corresponding to the fixed-income or stable dividend value of the stock and 50 yen corresponding to the value of the preemptive right. The next morning the price of the stock would drop to 100 yen and the right would lose value for the time being. It should be noted that the preemptive right can be exercised each time the company makes additional issues of equity as long as this system continues.

This analysis leads us to the conclusion that, in the traditional Japanese system, common stocks were effectively transmuted into quasi-fixed-income securities like preferred stocks, with a unique option feature represented by the preemptive right to par issues of additional stocks in the future. The floor value of these stocks was given by stable dividend flows discounted by opportunity cost based on the bank deposit rate, with added value reflecting the expectation of future new issues at par.

Until about 1980 small investors, who accounted for only a small proportion of the outstanding stocks, were the primary active investors in the secondary stock market. For them, unlike for major relationship corporate shareholders, for whom the theoretical value was 50 yen or so, common stocks with these unique features were worth much more than par value. Since for most of the time the actual market price of virtually all stocks was above par value, a new equity issue was almost always a positive factor for any stock. Thus in those days the expectation of an additional equity issue was a major plus factor for the price of stock.

Figure 7.2 represents a typical stock price pattern over time during phase one. When the market expects no new right issue in the near future, the price is based on the expectation of stable dividends and the prevailing interest rate, plus some discounted value for future right issues at par. When the next new right offering becomes a reality, the market starts to reflect fully the value of the right and the price of the stock rises sharply to reach the theoretical cum-right price (price

Historical stock prices of Toho Bank, a local commercial bank based in Fukushima Prefecture, between 1975 and 1984.

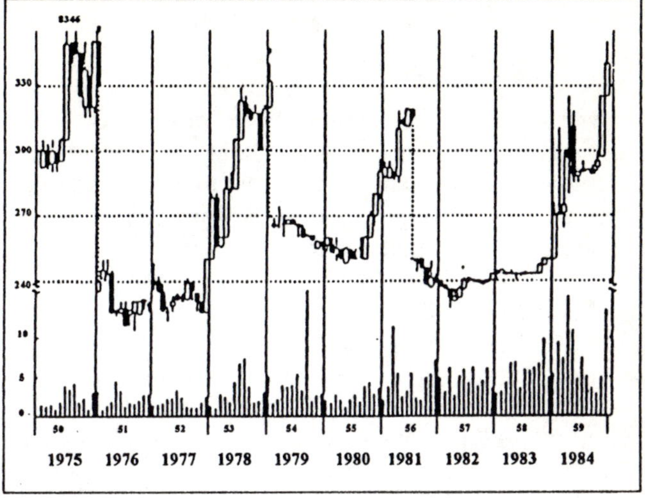

Source: 1985 Nen Kabuka Sōran, (Tokyo, Toyo Keizai Shinposha 1985)

FIGURE 7.2 Typical stock price pattern during phase one

including the proper premium in the right) by the day prior to its expiry.

Now, why did the average stock price of many companies fall into the 200–300 yen range in those years rather than 100 yen? The average dividend for all companies was somewhat higher than five yen, as shown in Figure 7.1, because five yen was considered the minimum acceptable amount during normal times. Another possibility was that the opportunity cost of small investors was less than 5 per cent if we consider that stocks were much more liquid than bank deposits. If we take bank, sight deposits accounts as an alternative to stock investment, the interest rate on these was much lower than for one-year term deposits. If the opportunity cost of investment was, say, 3 per cent, a five-yen cash flow every year in perpetuity would have value of 167 yen rather than 100 yen.

But probably the most important reason for average stock prices being much higher than 100 yen was the expectation of several new issues in the near future. If a one-to-one new issue creates a 50 yen value for the preemptive right, the expectation of two or more new issues in the foreseeable future will create significantly more value for this right. Remember the number of rights grows as more new issues are made. If you can reasonably expect that there will be two one-to-one new right offerings at par in the coming two years, one current share will increase to four shares in two years. In this case the theoretical present value of one share with a fixed dividend value of 100 yen is something like 227 yen if discounted at 5 per cent.

The fact that the average stock price was in the 200–300 yen range in those days suggests that the market on average reflected an expectation of two one-to-one rights issues in the foreseeable future.

It should be noted that under the par issue system, growth was given to shareholders not in terms of higher earnings per share or dividends per share over time, but in terms of an increased number of shares, each of which was essentially fixed income in nature. For relatively uninformed and unsophisticated individual investors, it was not realistic to anticipate more than two or three right offerings in the foreseeable future, and a stock price of more than 500 yen or so could not be justified.

However this kind of stock market was ideal for the main banks as major relationship shareholders. Since the market stock prices of virtually all companies were well above par value, the normal book cost of equity investment for the main banks, this system guaranteed the 'unrealised capital gain' on their relationship equity investment portfolio. The unrealised capital gain was regarded as a major cushion for the risk associated with the main banks' responsibility to commit a capital package to their client companies regardless of their financial performance. This system also enabled the main banks to accommodate comfortably the ever growing capital needs, both debt and equity, of their client companies during the era of high economic growth because the par issue system guaranteed the unrealised gain whenever the main banks subscribed to additional equity issues.

The last point about the old system was the importance of the use of a small-scale a limited free distribution of shares, typically 0.05 to 0.1, shares per one share with new rights issues. In the case of 0.1 free distribution on the occasion of a one-to-one new issue, each existing shareholder could purchase one new share for only 45 yen, or 90 per cent of the par value.

In Western investment theory, free distribution is merely a form of stock splitting, and while the number of shares increases, the share price drops accordingly so the overall effect is neutral, except that it often results in a small change (increase) in dividends.

In the Japanese system this was not the case. Since the company committed itself to paying the same fixed dividend for those free shares too, they clearly had a fixed-income value as well as a rights value. If the fixed-income value of one share was 100 yen, 0.1 free distribution meant the company was giving away something that was worth ten yen.

Moreover, for the stable relationship shareholders, including the main banks, for whom the cost of investment was always recognised as the average paid-in historical book cost, free distribution effectively reduced the average book cost of investment, or denominator, while at the same time contributing to an increase in dividend income on the indicator side, effectively improving the dividend yield on the average book cost of investment. Free distribution was always welcomed by relationship corporate investors and individual outside investors alike.

8 Stock Valuation in Japan: Phase Two

8.1 THE PROLIFERATION OF NEW EQUITY FINANCING AT MARKET PRICE

As shown in Table 6.5, virtually all new equity financing came to be made through public offerings at market price after early 1980s. However, the amount of pure equity financing remained modest for most years, and since new equity issues were offered at much higher prices than under the old system, the increase in the number of outstanding shares was marginal. Also, it should be noted that, especially during the 1980s, convertible bonds and bonds with warrants as a vehicle of equity financing were heavily used as an alternative to pure equity financing. The amount of financing through convertible bonds and bonds with warrants in the domestic and overseas markets amounted to 38 trillion yen during 1986–89, taking advantage of the very high stock prices that prevailed during the bubble years.

The concept of publicly offering new equities at market price to all investors, relationship or spot, was in outright conflict with the traditional relationship-based financial system. This idea was first tried by companies in industries that had low priority in the traditional capital allocation system. The first major example was the Yamaha Corporation (formerly Nippon Musical Instrument), which was classified under 'miscellaneous manufacturing industries' in the Tokyo Stock Exchange. Then many young and fast-growing companies, including chainstore and franchise operations in the retail or fast food business, started to enter this attractive new area of risk capital. These new companies typically did not enjoy the luxury of relationships with the main banks and therefore had no access to the traditional pool of debt and equity capital. These companies represented the high-risk, high-return segment of the capital market and investors in these stocks for the first time bore the full residual risk of the companies. Hence this marked the beginning of the development of a pure common stock market in Japan.

One of the big attractions of this new method of equity financing was the fact that the portion of cash flow that leaked out of the operation of companies in the form of dividends as a percentage of the amount raised was, at least in the short run, drastically reduced compared with the old system. Whereas this portion had been at least 10 per cent under the old system, it came down to 1 per cent or even less. This aspect of the new method of equity financing was exactly what emerging, fast-growing companies needed. The problem was, this feature also attracted many large, established companies in the high-priority industries, which already enjoyed the full benefits of the traditional financial system, including main bank relations. Because these low-risk, low-return companies gradually adopted the new method and came to be valued on the basis of expected constant growth, their stock prices shifted from the traditional low levels based on fixed dividends to levels similar to those of the high-risk, high-return group.

The timing of this shift varied from one company or industry to another. Figure 8.1 shows how and when selected companies made this shift over time. Some, for example Ito Yokado and Sony, from the very beginning raised capital by offering shares to the public at market price. Therefore their stock prices were valued at well over 1000 yen from the very early stage. Then Toyota, which did not belong to any established group and was financially independent from the banking system, came to be valued by the US standard as Toyota stock became highly favoured among foreign investors during the 1970s. In the early 1980s some major established electric and electronic companies, including Hitachi and NEC, made this shift. By the middle of the 1980s many more established companies with main banks had followed suit. Towards the peak of the bubble economy in the late 1980s, banks, securities companies, electric utilities and major steel companies made the shift. By the end of the 1980s this gradual shift in stock valuation in Japan from phase one to phase two had been completed.

The public offering of new shares at market price contradicted with what had happened to the corporate financing system in the 1970s. As Japan was to join the IMF Article 8 countries in the early 1970s, it was preparing to open up its capital market to the rest of the world, which included the liberalisation of M & A (mergers and acquisitions) through tender offers by foreign companies. In fact Japanese companies so feared the possibility of takeover bids by foreign companies that they began to strengthen their relationships with the main banks, other financial institutions, other group companies and subcontractors so that the majority of their outstanding shares could be securely held or cross-held by friendly corporate investors. As a result of this effort the proportion of stocks held stably and cross-held showed a marked increase during the 1970s. Thus relationship financing strengthened rather than weakened after the new equity financing shifted from par value to the market price system. As a result the role of the main banks as lender of last resort of both debt and equity capital became even more important for most companies, including young and high-growth companies.

Reflecting this trend, the net addition of relationship equity investment by major banks accelerated on the book basis during the 1980s (Table 8.1). Until the end of the 1970s the basic principle of the major banks' equity relationship investment was to keep them well within their equity amount or net worth on the book basis. During the unprecedented equity financing boom in the 1980s, this principle was eroded and the major banks provided more equity capital than their own equity financing, which also amounted to a phenomenal sum.

The shift of major established companies from rights offerings at par to market price meant an outright breach of the

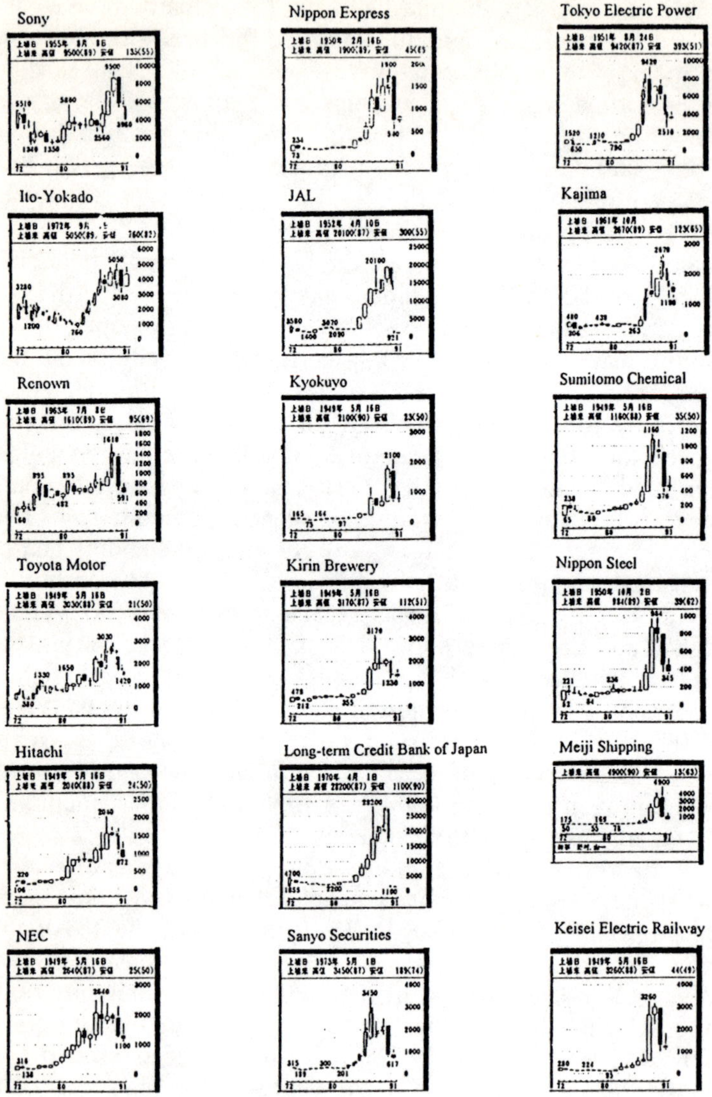

Source: Chart Book, No. 869 (Tokyo, Toshi Radar Inc., 1992)

FIGURE 8.1 Long-term stock price trend of selected issues

TABLE 8.1 Amount of relationship equity investment by the major city banks (book value)

Year ending March	*Total amount of equity investment (trillion yen)*	*Banks' net worth (trillion yen)*
1966	0.4	0.4
1976	2.0	2.6
1981	3.8	3.3
1986	6.7	5.2
1989	13.2	10.3
1990	16.9	13.7

Source: Nomura Research Institute.

tacit but fundamental premise of the traditional financial system. For stable relationship investors, including the main banks, which continued to be approached to maintain a stable fraction of the ownership of client companies even under the new system, it meant at least a marginally sharp rise in the average cost of equity investment, effectively reducing the average dividend yield on their investment portfolios. This was especially serious for life insurance companies, which relied heavily on dividend income. And for all relationship financial institutions the shift triggered a slow but steady process of 'marking to market' the average cost of stock investment. This problem materialised in a dramatic manner during 1990–92 after the stock market collapse, because the major decline in stock prices coupled with the increased average book cost of investment almost wiped out the unrealised capital gains on the stock portfolios of the major banks, which came very close to failing to meet the Bank for International Settlements' new bank equity rule of 8 per cent.

Borrowing companies tried to alleviate this problem by introducing a voluntary programme to distribute systematically to existing shareholders the surplus capital raised through new issues of stocks at market price, in the form of free distributions of stocks on a regular basis, while at the same time promising to maintain stable dividends per share. This programme reduced the average book cost of stock investments for relationship investors while increasing the dividend received.

The program was an effort to incorporate the new method of equity financing at market price into the traditional relationship-based financial system, but as more and more established companies adopted the new method it became clear that this strategy would not work over a long run.

The problem was especially serious for the main banks, for whom the automatic increase of unrealised capital gains on their relationship stock investments offered a cushion against the risks arising from their commitment to capital-hungry company clients, because the new system meant there would longer no be a guarantee of unrealised capital gains for any new equity financing. Consequently, to maintain the relationship-based financial system a more fundamental solution was needed. And the solution was to build in or strengthen the various mechanisms whose combined effect was to limit the downside risk of the stock market while leaving the upward potentials wide open, by creating an 'ever rising' stock market during the 1980s. Under a strong rising trend in the stock market there could be no capital loss for any stable long-term investors, no matter when or at what price they subscribed to new equity issues for their client companies. If this condition was met the main banks could continue to act as stable shareholders, maintaining a fixed fraction of ownership under the new equity financing system without the fear that temporary declines in the stock price would create even marginal capital losses.

The former relationship-based financial system demanded the transformation of common stocks into some sort of quasi-fixed-income securities with the right or option to subscribe to any new equity issues at par. Under the new system it demanded the creation of a secondary stock market where stocks were priced as if they were long-term call options based on common stocks, rather than pure common stocks.

8.2 STOCK VALUATION DURING PHASE TWO

To the extent that the holders of common stock are protected against loss beyond losing the invested amount, common stock is clearly a kind of option security. In any reasonably well-developed stock market, short-term changes in stock prices tend to conform to normal distribution in the statistical sense, and long-term changes to log-normal distribution. At any rate, the possibility of a negative return on investment constitutes the major risk of investing in common stock. In Japan, however, because large bank shareholders, 95 per cent or more of whose capital structure consists of deposit, or short-term, fixed-charge liability, can not afford to accept such a risk, various efforts have been made to restrict or eliminate the downside risk of investing in common stock[5]. Because the performance of banks and other major financial institutions is measured and supervised on an annual book or average-historical-cost basis, it is essential to provide a hedge against the possibility of capital loss or of the market price of stocks declining below their book cost at the end of any reporting period. Once banks suffer a capital loss they have to report the loss immediately on their profit and loss statements and they must produce income to make up for the loss if their operating profit is not large enough to cover it. If such a loss materialises in the course of normal cyclical ups and downs in the stock market, banks cannot remain major, stable shareholders without seriously jeopardising their main business of commercial and industrial lending. This was exactly what happened to Japanese banks, then under the newly introduced BIS bank equity rule, in the early 1990s when the stock market declined sharply.

In the US system the primary risk of investment is defined as the degree to which the realised return may deviate from the expected return, and is statistically measured by the standard deviation of the return distribution. Whether or not the return is negative (less than zero per cent) is of secondary importance because the performance of professional investment managers is usually evaluated against relevant benchmarks. In Japan the risk of a market price dropping below the average book cost of investment is perceived as the primary risk of investment by the main banks and other relationship investors.

Studying a major Japanese stock price index can provide us with some evidence of the call-optionisation of the Japanese stock market after the mid 1970s. Figure 8.2 shows the result of a buy-and-hold investment strategy for a broadly based market portfolio for 6, 12 and 24 months, conducted month by month, starting on 1 January 1974 and ending on 31 December, 1989. The distribution of the annual percentage change of the portfolio's value (excluding dividend receipts) was measured for each of the three holding periods. For purposes of comparison, the same analysis was conducted for the United States using the S & P 500 index as a proxy for the market portfolio. Based on this analysis, we can point out the following characteristics of the Japanese market compared with the stock price pattern in the United States.

1. For a six-month holding period, the distribution of price changes in both nations showed relatively small skewness and could still be approximated by a normal bell shape.
2. For a 12-month holding period, the negative changes were only 15 tries out of 181 in Japan compared with 48 trials in the United States. Moreover the biggest negative change during this period in Japan was 17.05 per cent while the average realised change was plus 15.20 per cent. The downside price risk for Japanese investors was already pretty well eliminated for the holding period of 12 months. This was not at all the case in the United States.
3. If the holding period was 24 months or longer, which was normally the case with most Japanese relationship investors, the downside price risk was completely eliminated or hedged during these 15 years. Of the 156 trials covering the 24-month holding period, on no occasion did the final portfolio value fall below the initial investment value or the historical cost of investment. Of course in any market, including the United States average returns show a positive skewness as the holding period becomes longer.

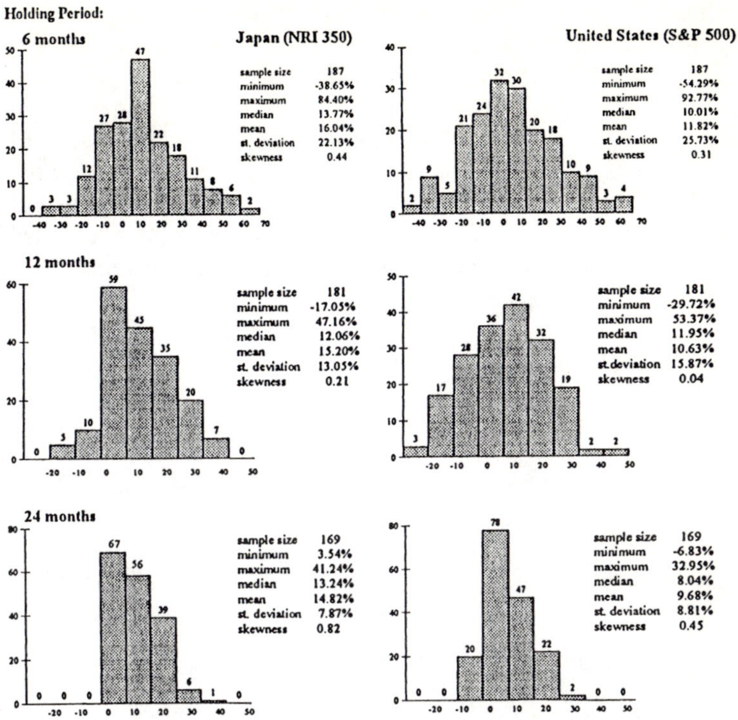

Source: Nomura Research Institute.

FIGURE 8.2 Stock price changes in Japan and the United States (January 1974 to December 1989)

As a result the skewness statistics for the United States for the 24-month period rose from 0.04 to 0.45 over the 12-month period. Still there were 20 negative changes. Six negative changes were observed even if the holding period was extended to 36 months in the United States during those years.

The above study shows that, at least from 1974–89, the Japanese stock market behaved as if it was a call option market based on stocks rather than a typical market for common stocks. It was often asserted that investment in a broadly diversified stock portfolio in Japan was free from negative returns for investment periods of more than three years, but the above study suggests that two years was long enough. It was not a coincidence that many Japanese stock investment funds have a two-year non-refund clause. The strong sales appeal of Japanese stock trust funds was that they were effectively hedged against downside risk and had a large upward potential, which was very similar to a stock call option.

9 Factors Underpinning the Call-Optionisation of the Stock Market

9.1 THE DOWNSIDE RISK HEDGING SYSTEM

First I would like to discuss some of the factors that underpinned the development of the call-option type of stock market during phase two. Since hedging against the downside risk of stock investment was a system-wide effort, both formal and informal, it is impossible to provide a complete list of the factors that contributed to it. However at its roots were the built-in stabilisers of the entire postwar economic system of Japan, which enabled it to manage and control its major macro policy parameters, including the inflation rate, interest rate, cost of capital, unemployment, national budget, international balance of payments and so on. The following are a few of the important factors:

1. There was a general consensus that price stability, and especially the prevention of severe drops in price, was desirable.
2. The main banks acted as lenders of last resort, and there was a broad consensus that major listed companies should not be allowed to go bankrupt.
3. Large securities companies acted as floor members of major stock exchanges, and when necessary mobilized all their resources to stabilise the market.
4. A mechanism was put in place to allow 'wash sales' in order to neutralise the impact on the market of sales of

large blocks of stocks by the major banks (called 'cross-trading') primarily for the purpose of realising capital gains on stock portfolios to boost accounting profits for reporting purposes.
5. There was no means, such as stock index futures and options, to systematically bet against the market.
6. There was a strong government commitment to maintain the stock price index at a certain level, as evidenced by the widely publicised official and informal efforts by the Ministry of Finance that, as a package, came to be known as 'price-keeping operations' (PKOs).

All of these effectively limited the downside risk of stock investment, especially for investors whose investment horizon was longer than one year.

9.2 THE NATURE OF THE 'JAPANESE BEAUTY CONTEST'

Next we shall consider why there was an ever-rising stock price trend during the 1970s and 1980s despite the fact that corporate profitability continued to decline throughout these two decades. In US capitalism, stock prices are expected to start to decline as soon as the market perceives the prospect of declining profitability measured by, among other things, return on equity (ROE).

The key to understanding the Japanese puzzle seems to lie in the type of 'beauty contest' people engaged in during those years. Instead of basing their decisions on ROE, the productivity of shareholders' capital, or the growth of earnings and/or dividends per share, Japanese investors primarily based them on the growth prospects of the aggregate profits of major companies. As shown in Figure 9.1, the aggregate profits of major industrial and commercial companies continued to grow, with temporary cyclical falls in 1982–83 and 1985–86, while the average ROE continued to decline over the two decades.

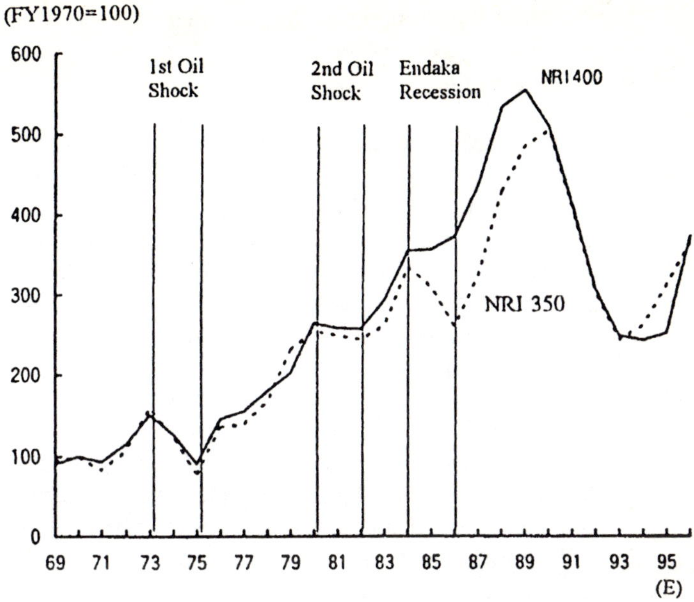

Source: NRI News Release (Tokyo: Nomura Research Institute, 1995)

FIGURE 9.1 Trend of recurring profits

In order to analyse the nature of the 'beauty contest', we undertook an empirical study to try to find out which financial numbers and ratios were most relevant to investment performance during the 1980s.

9.2.1 The Empirical Evidence

For this analysis the following fundamental variables were chosen to correlate the investment performance of Japanese stocks:

1. Rate of change in sales.
2. Rate of change in recurring profits.

3. Rate of change in recurring profits per share.
4. Rate of change in net income.
5. Rate of change in net income per share.

Sales and profits were chosen in order to ascertain whether the level of operations or the level of profits had the greater effect on stock prices. Recurring profits and net income were chosen in order to ascertain which of these benchmarks on profits had the greater influence on the stock price. Recurring profits and net income per share were added to the analysis in order to ascertain whether total earnings or earnings per share had the greater influence on stock prices.[1]

For the period 1980–90, 483 corporations were studied. All were listed in the first section of the Tokyo Stock Exchange and their fiscal year always ended in March. Each of these firms' total returns for the ten fiscal years between 1981 and 1990 were subject to regression analysis in relation to the above fundamental indicators. For instance, in order to obtain a correlation between recurring profits and the rate of return on stock, for the first year, (from the end of March 1980 to the end of March 1981) each stock's rate of return was regressed against the rate of change of recurring profits the same year. The analysis was repeated for the remaining nine years, including the fiscal year ending March 1990. The results of this analysis are summarised in Table 9.1.

The major findings are as follows.

First, for each of the profit indicators – not only for the ten-year average but also for each of the ten years – the regression coefficient and correlation coefficient were positive. This means that the rate of return on stocks with a high profit growth rate tended to be higher. The *t* value on all profit indicators exceeded 2.0 for each of the years; this correlation is statistically significant.

However the coefficient of determination (the square of the correlation coefficient) was less than 0.1 for the average value for each of the indicators for the ten-year period. This reflects the fact that numerous factors other than the fundamentals were affecting stock prices, and that profits accounted for less

TABLE 9.1 Regression analysis in relation to fundamental variables and realised total return in Japan*

	Regression coefficient	*t-value*	*Number of years when $t > 2$*	*Correlation coefficient*
Rate of change in sales	0.560	3.110	5	0.158
Rate of change in recurring profits	0.258	5.515	10	0.254
Rate of change in recurring profits per share	0.234	4.912	10	0.227
Rate of change in net income	0.307	4.735	10	0.224
Rate of change in net income per share	0.205	4.240	10	0.195

* 10 year average.

Source: Fumio Takahashi, 'Fundamental Information and Stock Price Formation in Japan', *Security Analysts Journal*, May 1991 (The Security Analysts Association of Japan).

were affecting stock prices, and that profits accounted for less than 10 per cent of the variation in the return on stocks.

Second, In the case of sales the *t* value exceeded 2.0 for five years only. This means that its influence on stock prices was comparatively less than in the case of profits. Hence it is evident that it was not the expansion of a firm's scale of operation, but the increase of its profits that affected the price of its shares.

Third, in comparing the respective effects of recurring profits and net income, the former offered a better explanation of share price than the latter on the basis of both total profits and profits per share, when the data for the final eight of the ten years covered by this analysis were taken into consideration. According to Japan's accounting practices, recurring profits rather than net income do indeed better express the changing pattern of a firm's real profits. Hence recurring profits are used more frequently as a firm's indicator of profits.

Finally, apart from the fiscal year ending March 1985, on the basis of both recurring profits and net income, total profits served better than profits per share in explaining the per share price; in other words, total profits had a greater influence on the stock price than profits per share.

Next the same 483 companies were classified into five groups, ranked in descending order of recurring profits, which are thought to be most highly correlated with stock return. A portfolio of each group of stocks was formed, where each of the stocks were given the same weight, and each portfolio's rate of return for all ten years was calculated. Then, assuming that investment continued for each of the ranked portfolios, the difference in their performance was calculated. The results of the simulation are shown in Table 9.2 and Figure 9.2.

As Table 9.2a shows, apart from fiscal years ending March 1985 and 1989, the higher the growth rate of the recurring profits of the portfolio stocks, the higher their rate of return. Consequently the higher the growth of profitability of a portfolio containing higher-growth stocks, the greater its ten-year average return. For instance, when continual investment was made in the highest ranking portfolio, comprising stocks recording the highest growth of annual profits, an average return of 41.8 per cent could be obtained. On the other hand, if continual investment was made in the lowest- or fifth-ranking portfolio, comprising stocks recording the lowest growth of annual profits, the average return would have been only 7.5 per cent.

Table 9.2b and Figure 9.2 show the cumulative value of each of the portfolios. The value of the highest-ranking portfolio would have increased from 100 to 2901.5 at the end of 10 years, while that of the fifth-ranking portfolio would have only grown to 192.5, producing a large performance gap between the two portfolios over the ten-year period.

Despite the low correlation of 0.254 obtained between the growth rate of recurring profits and the rate of return on the stocks in the ten-year period, it is obvious that the investment performance of portfolios with higher profit growth rates was better than those with lower profit growth rates. This is noteworthy from a pragmatic viewpoint on portfolio investment.

A comparative analysis of the US stock market was also made in order to verify whether the foregoing correlation between a corporation's fundamental indicators and its stock price is unique to the Japanese stock market.[2]

For the US analysis, 667 corporations whose fiscal year ended in December were chosen from the Global-Vantage database. The analysis covered the eight-year period 1982–90. The method of analysis used was the same as that for Japan. For each calendar year a regression analysis was conducted for each stock's rate of return on the corporations' fundamental indicators (sales, net income and earnings per share). Also, a simulation was made of each stock's earnings per share, which would most cogently explain its rate of return. The analysis revealed that the return on US stocks was affected by corporate fundamentals, as in the case of Japan. In all years but 1984 the rate of return was higher for the group comprising stocks with higher profit growth. On the other hand, the following differences were noted between the Japanese and US markets:

TABLE 9.2 Stimulation results on recurring profits

	1981/3	*1982/3*	*1983/3*	*1984/3*	*1985/3*	*1986/3*	*1987/3*	*1988/3*	*1989/3*	*1990/3*	*Average*	*S.D.*
(a) *Rate of return* (%)												
1st rank	39.0	4.7	33.5	80.3	20.8	66.6	39.4	61.9	49.6	21.9	41.8	23.2
2nd rank	21.7	1.7	20.4	62.4	15.4	47.2	37.1	45.4	35.6	13.2	30.0	18.6
3rd rank	21.5	–3.8	17.8	39.1	11.0	45.0	23.7	45.0	31.3	6.7	23.7	16.5
4th rank	13.6	–4.6	7.5	27.2	12.2	28.0	9.5	42.7	19.3	0.7	15.6	14.1
5th rank	–2.1	–6.0	–0.4	16.9	8.8	16.8	–6.5	24.2	27.4	–4.5	7.5	13.0

	1980/3	*1981/3*	*1982/3*	*1983/3*	*1984/3*	*1985/3*	*1986/3*	*1987/3*	*1988/3*	*1989/3*	*1990/3*
(b) *Cumulative value*											
1st rank	100	139.0	145.5	194.3	350.3	423.2	705.0	982.8	1591.1	2380.2	2901.5
2nd rank	100	121.7	123.8	149.0	242.0	279.3	411.1	563.6	819.5	1111.2	1257.9
3rd rank	100	121.5	116.9	137.7	191.5	212.6	308.3	381.3	552.9	726.0	774.6
4th rank	100	113.6	108.4	116.5	148.2	166.3	212.8	233.0	332.6	396.7	399.5
5th rank	100	97.9	92.0	91.7	107.1	116.6	136.2	127.3	158.1	201.4	192.4

Source: See Table 9.1.

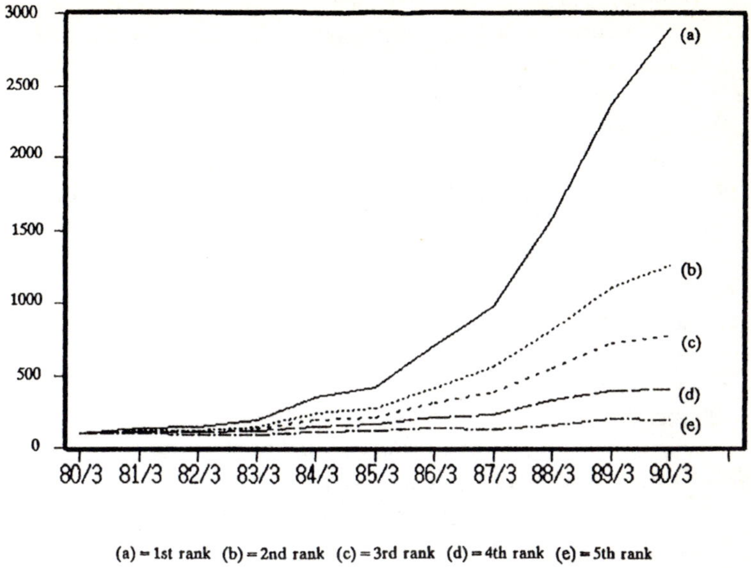

Source: See Table 9.1.

FIGURE 9.2 Cumulative value of ranking portfolio

1. Analysis of the *t* value and correlation coefficient indicates that the US stocks were more influenced by corporate fundamentals.
2. The US market differed from Japan's in that earnings per share rather than net income had the greater influence on stock profitability.
3. The *t* value and correlation coefficient indicates that in the United States the rate of change of sales had a greater influence on the stock price than in Japan. In other words, on the whole the correlation between sales and profits was greater and the profit margin more stable in the United States than in Japan. This could be attributed to the fact that US corporations tend to prefer stable profits, and are

inclined to opt aggressively for diversification and divestiture of unprofitable operations, while Japanese corporations tend to maintain a greater number of deficit-ridden and unprofitable operations.

9.3 RECONCILIATION OF THE CALL-OPTIONISED MARKET WITH FINANCE THEORY

One way of interpreting the above findings is that the Japanese 'beauty contest' concerned with a *relative* valuation (not *absolute* valuation), based on the aggregate rather than per-share profit.

The call-optionised stock market did not develop according to a careful plan, but rather just happened after the fixed dividend constraint was removed during the 1970s and some companies started to offer shares at the market price. Probably the most serious flaw in the Japanese stock market was that it totally lacked a system or group of investors to bet against the market, as well as to arbitrage between the current market price and a theoretical fundamental value. As long as stock prices continued to rise, all investors, relationship or not, as well as the brokerage and underwriting industry and the government, were happy with it. There were absolutely no investors who cared about or had an incentive to question the underlying values of overpriced stocks during those years.

A call option, as compared with a common stock, typically has the following characteristics.

1. Holders of a call option do not question whether the price of the underlying asset (in this case a common stock) is higher or lower than its fundamental value.
2. The higher the price of the underlying asset, namely the common stock, the more valuable the call option.
3. With the downside risk effectively hedged, increased volatility is a positive rather than a negative factor.

9.4 THE ROLE OF MAIN BANKS AS THE DELEGATED MONITORS OF THE STOCK MARKET

In the call-optionised stock market the main banks play a key role as major relationship shareholders. As long-term, stable shareholders, however, the main banks have been unable to play an active role in the pricing of stocks; this has been the role of general, outside investors. However, as well-informed insiders underwriting the health of borrowing companies through their commitment to remaining stable shareholders (or de facto business partners), large banks have been able to act as 'delegated monitors' for outside investors.

In the area of lending, the role of the main banks as delegated monitors is a well-accepted concept. Representing the group of lenders, the main banks are typically expected to monitor the business and financial performances of borrowing companies, assess their creditworthiness and new investment projects, and commit further financial and managerial resources when a firm experiences financial distress.[3] If the main banks, as delegated monitors, can play a valuable role in the lending market, which consists of a relatively small number of well-trained and sophisticated professional managers, it is clear that they could play an even more valuable role in the stock market, which consists of a large number of relatively unsophisticated, small public investors.

The major roles of the main banks as the delegated monitors of the stock market can be summarised as follows:

1. The main banks have developed long-term, interlocking business relations with many important companies whose stocks are listed on major stock exchanges, assuming, in many cases, the position of *de facto* business partners rather than 'arms'-length' investors or creditors.
2. They monitor the health of client companies not as neutral, third-party agencies like bond rating agencies or security analysts, but as business partners of last resort, so

they are committed to providing further managerial and financial resources should their client companies get into financial or operational difficulty.

3. Unlike US institutional shareholders, who typically sell off shares as soon as they receive adverse information about the companies concerned, the main banks are expected to remain stable shareholders and often increase their commitment if it is requested, the opposite behaviour to that normally required for efficient stock pricing.
4. The main banks are *de facto* insiders regarding fundamental information about client companies, and the asymmetry of information between the main banks and other investors is even more significant than in the case of the lending market.

US capitalism, in which arms-length, pure financial investment is the norm, aimed for the development of an efficient stock market based on the requirement for public disclosure of fundamental corporate information, together with a large number of investment professionals to act as agents of the citizen at large. For Japan, where these conditions were not in place and the economy was in the throes of catching up, the use of main banks as major stable shareholders was a very practical approach. In the call-optionised stock market the main banks are expected to monitor the health of companies as well-informed and deeply committed 'insider' investors.

How, then, does the market receive assurance from the main banks? The key requirement is that the main banks will remain committed, stable shareholders. More specifically, outside investors feel comfortable as long as the main banks' percentage ownership of companies remains stable or increases rather than declines. This does not mean that the banks and other relationship shareholders should not and never will sell their investments. In fact, they have occasionally sold some relationship investment shares in the market when it was necessary for them to realise capital gains for financial reporting purposes, and capital gains have been the main source of extraordinary income for banks when faced with the need to write off large bad loans. In the event of such sales, however, the banks have almost always bought back the same number of shares of the same companies essentially at the same prices through the same brokerage house by means of so-called 'cross-transactions'.

In the United States this type of transaction is called a 'wash sale' and is banned by law because it is a disguised form of tax evasion. In Japan it has been accepted and openly publicised. It is well known that towards the end of the reporting period (March and September), when banks close their books for auditing by the Ministry of Finance and the Bank of Japan, the trading volumes in the Osaka and Nagoya Stock Exchanges surge in response to cross-transactions by banks. One reason why this practice has been openly reported until today is that the market wants assurance that the banks are selling part of their relationship investment merely for technical reasons. The announcement of a cross-transaction conveys the message to the market that the sale is not based on any fundamental reasons and that the banks are committed to maintaining their stable ownership positions.

Until the early 1990s bank equity holding continued to increase, at least on a book-value basis, even after the banks started to sell shares in a major way in order to write off the huge bad loans that materialised when the economic bubble burst. Even though most of the recent sales have been cross-transactions rather than outright sales, the average cost of investment has been gradually 'marked-to-market' through such selling. To date there has been no major evidence that the main banks have begun to withdraw their commitment as shareholders of last resort. However, with the new BIS bank equity rule, greatly reduced share prices and a gradual increase in the average cost of investment, the role of the main banks as stable shareholders may well have started to decline.

9.5 SUMMARY

Until it crashed in 1990 the Japanese stock market was designed in such a way that price changes would conform more to the pattern of option securities than to that of pure common stocks. In the first half of the postwar period the market valued stocks as if they were quasi-fixed-income securities with warrants, and in the second half as if they were call options based on common stocks. The long-term experience was such that most investors naturally assumed that the stock market would continue to rise, with little downside risk. Virtually all the parties involved – relationship and outside investors, stockbrokers, banks and other financial institutions, borrowing companies and the government – benefited from the ever-rising stock market, and there was strong agreement that the higher the stock price, the better it was for everybody. As will be discussed in Part III, the high stock prices reduced the cost of equity capital and further strengthened the competitiveness of Japanese companies in the export market. Until stock index futures and options were introduced in the late 1980s, few investors would have benefited from a stock price decline, nor was it possible to short-sell the market even if stocks were grossly overpriced. The market crash brought about a belated adjustment, and stock prices were pulled more into line with their fundamental value.

The following are unique features of the Japanese stock market:

1. The main banks and other major financial institutions, whose chief business has been to accept deposit-type savings and lend them to industrial and commercial companies, have occupied the position of holders of both senior debt and common stocks as a package, fully bearing the residual risks of the borrowing companies.
2. Outside investors have held and traded, not pure common stocks, but quasi-fixed-income securities (similar to preferred stock) with some kind of option feature and without the residual risk inherent in any pure common stock.

3. A secondary market for pure common stocks bearing full residual risk and voting rights has not developed to any significant degree. This is evidenced by the total lack of open-mergers, acquisitions and takeover activities through the Japanese stock market even today.

Part III

Corporate Profitability and the Cost of Capital

10 Corporate Profitability and International Competition

10.1 THE CORPORATE FINANCING SYSTEM AS THE CORE OF THE 'BETTER AND CHEAPER' STRATEGY

After the Second World War the Japanese economic system achieved consistently high growth, and aggressive investment in plant and equipment by the manufacturing sector was the main engine of the growth. Therefore reducing the cost of capital, a key factor in the investment decisions by the companies, was critical for Japan's pursuit of growth.

In the value-creation cycle shown in Figure 2.1, Japan did not regard the interest rate (or cost of debt) and the required return by shareholders (or cost of equity) as something that should be left to the market mechanism and beyond the control of the managers of the nation's economy. In a developmental economy such as postwar Japan, the idea of managing or controlling the interest rate and the required return on equity capital was consistent with the idea of strategic allocation of resources. In fact until the early 1970s Japan openly maintained a low interest rate policy to promote the international competitiveness of important industries and companies. Although Japan was not the only country to adopt this strategy, it was one of the few to do it so extensively and systematically.

A system that effectively reduces the cost of equity capital to below that which would prevail in an open market offers additional competitive advantages to the companies operating under it. As will be discussed in detail later, the unique features of Japan's capital market – such as the main bank system, stable stockholding and the cross-holding of stocks – made it possible for Japan's major companies substantially to reduce the cost of their equity capital. Because of these practices, which were inconceivable in the US financial system, large Japanese companies could procure equity capital at relatively low cost, irrespective of their financial performance or profitability, as conventionally defined.

Traditional macroeconomists estimate and compare the cost of capital among nations as a key determinant of the level of an economy's fixed capital asset formation – the lower the cost of capital, the higher the level of investment. In Japan, however, the precondition for sustained and intense investment activity was to establish and maintain a strong competitive position in the international open market for the major proportion of the ever-increasing manufactured output of these investment activities. Only if Japanese companies remained competitive in the international market would Japan continue to maintain a high level of investment in the value-creation cycle shown in Figure 2.1. Therefore the 'better and cheaper' approach became a common feature of the competitive behaviour of many export-oriented Japanese companies.

In the open market, where all resources are available to anyone at essentially the same price, no one will enjoy a major advantage in terms of cost, be it for labour, raw materials, technology, equipment or capital. However if a nation enjoys some structural advantage in the cost of one or more inputs in the value-creation process, the companies operating in this particular subsystem will enjoy a structural cost advantage when they compete in the open market. Japan's relatively well-educated, well-trained, hard-working, low-cost labour force compared with those in the United States and Europe immediately after the Second World War was the best example of such an advantage.

When the international open market system began to develop for raw materials, industrial goods and technology under the Bretton Woods regime, Japan, even though defeated in the war, was one of the world's leading industrial nations, and therefore was able to compete at the high end of the manufactured goods market from the beginning.

In 1950 the exchange rate was stabilised at 360 yen per US dollar, while before the war the ratio had been four to one. Japan's labour cost was roughly one fourth of that of the United States right after the war.[1] As a result Japanese companies could easily compete against their US counterparts by delivering good-quality manufactured goods at very low prices to the international marketplace. Japan's cheap, high-quality labour force and its stable and competitive new exchange rate under the open world economic system were probably the most important factors behind its rapid recovery from the devastation of the war and the miraculously high growth of its economy. However as Japan's success continued the wage rates started gradually to increase, and when the yen was revalued in the early 1970s, cheap labour was removed as a major competitive factor.

Until the early 1970s Japan suffered from a shortage of capital, in particular US dollars, the only hard currency accepted in the international market for raw materials and basic and advanced technologies, all of which were indispensable if Japan was to pursue its 'better and cheaper' strategy in the international manufactured goods sector. Thus hard currency had to be carefully allocated to high-priority projects and industries. During the 1950s and most of the 1960s the United States had very low inflation, very low interest rates and high stock prices (high PER). In other words US companies enjoyed very low cost of debt and equity. In contrast Japan had moderate inflation, higher interest rates and lower stock prices (low PER) compared with the United States (Table 10.1). This meant that the cost of capital for Japanese companies was significantly higher than for US companies. The main reason why Japan adopted a low interest rate policy and a 'low profitability strategy' was to minimise its cost-of-capital disadvantage relative to its major competitors in general and the United States in particular. According to many empirical studies, there is no evidence that Japan's capital costs were lower than those of the United States prior to 1980.

During the 1970s inflation in the United States accelerated and it became a nation of relatively high inflation, high interest rates and low stock prices. In contrast Japan began to experience lower inflation, lower interest rates and higher stock prices. By 1980 the United States' and Japan's relative cost-of-capital position had completely reversed. Thus cheap capital, both debt and equity, became Japan's main competitive factor during the 1970s and 1980s, replacing the cheap labour that had dominated during the 1950s and 1960s.

In this and following chapter I shall focus on corporate profitability, the cost of capital and international competition.

10.2 INTERNATIONAL COMPARISON OF CORPORATE PROFITABILITY

The cost of capital reflects the minimum return that the suppliers of capital – debt and equity – are willing to accept from borrowing companies. If we assume that the performance of a company is evaluated mainly on the basis of its business results, as reported in its financial statements, we can assume that the primary goal of the management of any listed company is to maintain sufficient profitability to satisfy the suppliers of capital.

In US capitalism the cost of capital is based on the current market price of debt securities and share prices. In the relationship-based Japanese capitalism the historical average book value has been the primary base of performance measurement, and therefore cost of capital has been conceived primarily in terms of required accounting profitability.

Referring back to Table 6.3, this simple table tells us two things:

1. Measured either by the after tax sales margin or ROE, Japan is the least profitable of the major industrial nations.

TABLE 10.1 Major market indicators United States and Japan, 1960–92

	Inflation (percentage change of CPI)		*Official discount rate (end of year) (%)*		*Long-term government bond yield (%)*		*Stock price (average PER)*		*Yen rate per dollar (Interbank)*
	USA	*Japan*	*USA*	*Japan*	*USA*	*Japan*	*USA*	*Japan*	
1960	1.6	3.1	3.53	6.94	4.0	–	17.7	NA	358
1965	1.7	7.8	4.04	5.48	4.2	–	16.8	NA	361
1970	5.9	7.7	5.50	6.00	7.4	–	16.5	9.9	358
1971	4.3	6.1	6.00	4.75	5.8	–	18.0	14.0	315
1972	3.3	4.5	4.50	4.25	6.7	–	18.0	18.9	302
1973	6.2	11.7	7.50	9.00	8.2	–	13.4	15.1	280
1974	11.0	24.4	7.75	9.00	8.4	–	9.4	17.6	301
1975	9.1	11.8	6.00	6.50	8.5	–	10.8	24.1	305
1976	5.8	9.3	5.25	6.50	8.6	–	10.4	21.6	293
1977	6.5	8.0	6.00	4.25	6.4	–	9.6	21.3	240
1978	7.7	3.8	9.50	3.50	6.4	6.4	8.2	21.2	195
1979	11.3	3.6	12.00	6.25	9.2	9.1	7.1	16.6	240
1980	13.5	8.0	13.00	7.25	8.9	8.8	8.4	18.1	203
1981	10.4	4.9	12.00	5.50	13.7	7.1	8.5	24.1	220
1982	6.1	2.7	8.50	5.50	10.5	7.9	10.4	22.4	242
1983	6.2	1.9	8.50	5.00	11.8	7.5	11.8	28.5	234
1984	4.3	2.4	8.00	5.00	11.5	6.7	9.9	26.2	248
1985	3.6	2.0	7.50	5.00	9.3	6.2	13.7	31.7	203

TABLE 10.1 *(Continued)*

	Inflation (percentage change of CPI)		*Official discount rate (end of year) (%)*		*Long-term government bond yield (%)*		*Stock price (average PER)*		*Yen rate per dollar (Interbank)*
	USA	*Japan*	*USA*	*Japan*	*USA*	*Japan*	*USA*	*Japan*	
1986	1.9	0.6	5.50	3.00	7.1	5.4	17.5	52.6	162
1987	3.6	0.1	6.00	2.50	8.9	5.1	16.0	56.8	128
1988	4.1	0.7	6.50	2.50	9.2	4.6	11.4	53.1	124
1989	4.8	2.3	7.00	4.25	7.9	5.8	13.6	49.9	144
1990	5.4	3.2	6.50	6.00	8.2	6.4	15.8	38.6	145
1991	3.1	2.7	4.50	4.50	6.9	5.5	25.6	39.7	135
1992	3.0	1.1	3.00	3.25	6.7	4.8	26.9	46.1	127

Source: *Economic Statistics Annual*, Bank of Japan, except for PERs, which are averages of high and low for the year for S&P Industrials for USA and NRI 350 for Japan.

2. In comparison with the stock markets in the other major nations, the Japanese stock market values the least profitable companies extremely highly.

These characteristics apply for almost all the years in the past two decades or so.

For a more detailed analysis, Table 10.2 compares the profitability of major companies in Japan and the United States. These data are averages based on actual results in the 1980s, obtained from the S & P index of industrial companies for the United States (some 400 companies) and the NRI 350 index of manufacturing and commercial companies for Japan. Data for the Japanese companies were compiled on a parent company basis.

To eliminate discrepancies in the calculation of profitability arising from differences in tax rates, capital structures or depreciation methods, the comparisons were made at four levels of the income statement: after-tax profit margin, pretax profit margin, operating profit margin and operating cash flow margin (the sum of operating profit plus depreciation as a percentage of sales). As a further check against distortion, the data for Japan are provided in two formats: including and the excluding the 10 large general trading companies, all of which have extremely low margins. The return on equity in the United States and Japan was then compared before and after tax.

Although some differences in degree are observable depending on the item under consideration, the data in Table 10.2 generally indicate that the profitability of Japanese companies was considerably lower than that of US companies. Specifically, US firms had an average return on equity of 13.9 per cent, compared with only 8.5 per cent for Japanese firms, while the pretax return on equity was 24.5 per cent for US companies but only 18.2 per cent for Japanese companies. The Japanese levels of return on equity changed only slightly when the general trading companies were included. If we assume that these averages reflect the minimum profitability levels that large corporations must maintain to continue

TABLE 10.2 Financial performance of the Japanese and US large-company sector (average percentage for 1980–88 financial year)

	Japan		*United States*
Profitability measure	*NRI 350*	*Ex. ten trading Companies*	*S&P Industrials*
Operating margin	3.2	5.2	9.8
(Operating income + depreciation)/sales	5.0	8.2	13.5
Pretax income/sales	2.8	4.6	8.0
Net income/sales	1.3	2.2	4.5
Return on equity			
Before tax	18.2	18.5	24.5
After tax	8.5	8.6	13.9

Sources: Nomura Research Institute; Standard & Poor. *NRI 400 Handbook* (Tokyo, Nomura Research Institute 1989) in *Japan: Standard & Poor's Analyst's Handbook* (New York, Standard & Poor's Corporation 1989)

operating as well-managed companies, the pretax cost of equity capital for large Japanese companies in the 1980s was roughly two thirds that of large US companies.

For a more precise comparison of the true profitability or required rate of return we have to adjust for many factors, including the inflation rate, accounting practices, the tax rate, cross-ownership effects, differences in capital structure and so on. Many studies indicate that even after careful adjustment for many of these factors, on average Japanese companies earned much less on their capital than US companies. Based on these observations, I conclude that Japanese companies have chosen to be much less profitable than US companies for competitive reasons. This conclusion is consistent with the basic characteristics of Japanese capitalism.

10.3 LOW PROFITABILITY AS AN INTERNATIONAL COMPETITIVE EDGE

Let us consider the implications for international competition if such a gap in required profitability between US and Japanese companies were to continue over a long period of time.

Based on the historical data in Table 10.2, Table 10.3 shows the minimum earnings before interest and tax (EBIT) that a large US and a large Japanese company would have to earn in order to invest a hypothetical 100 yen in new plant and equipment while still providing the minimum return expected by holders of the company's debt and equity capital, under the conditions that prevailed in the two markets during the 1980s. The calculation includes three new assumptions.

1. Reflecting the nominal interest rate differential between the United States and Japan in the 1980s, the interest rate on debt is set at 8 per cent for the former and 7 per cent for the latter.
2. The book equity to total capitalisation ratio is set at 50 per cent for US companies and 30 per cent for Japanese companies.
3. For ease of calculation the asset turnover rate for the new investment is set at one per year.

As Table 10.3 shows, in this hypothetical case the minimum that the US company must earn before interest and tax is 16.25 yen, compared with only 10.36 yen for the Japanese firm. This is almost 1.6 times more for the United States. Indeed US companies face a clear handicap of about six yen for each 100 yen of investment. Note too that a large part of the difference is attributable to the equity portion of the capital structure. This structural difference in the cost of capital would give Japanese companies a number of options when competing against US companies in the open market, including at least the following:

TABLE 10.3 Minimum required profitability of large Japanese and US industrial companies in the 1980s

	After tax (%)	*Pretax (%)*	*Weight*	*Minimum required EBIT*[1] *(%)*	*Yen*
US company:					
Debt (0.5)[2]		8.0	0.5	4.0	
Equity (0.5)[3]	13.9	24.5	0.5	12.25	
Total				16.25	16.25
Japanese company:					
Debt (0.7)[2]		7.0	0.7	4.9	
Equity (0.3)[3]	8.5	18.2	0.3	5.46	
Total				11.0	10.36

Notes: 1. Pretax profits multiplied by weight, or earnings before interest and tax (EBIT), assuming asset turnover of one per year.
2. Interest rate on debt set at 8 per cent for US companies and 7 per cent for Japanese companies.
3. Book equity to total capitalisation ratio set at 50 per cent for US companies and 30 per cent for Japanese companies.

Sources: See Table 10.2.

1. Lowering the selling price of their products.
2. Absorbing the high cost of importing raw materials and/or basic technologies not available in Japan.
3. Outspending their US rivals in aggressive capital investment (including the more frequent scrapping of existing plants and the building of new ones) and/or expanding R & D efforts.
4. Offering better quality products with additional functions without raising prices, or carrying out more aggressive advertising and sales promotion campaigns.
5. Maintaining employee morale and loyalty by avoiding layoffs, even at times when the workforce is overly large.
6. Making large-scale investments in businesses that have stable markets but offer only low returns – investments that US companies would find it difficult to justify.

7. Concentrating on mature product segments that earn low returns but have a stable market size, and which do not involve too much risk in terms of technology or marketing.
8. In situations where prices are set in the open market or where competitors' strategies are known, pursuing a strategy of undercutting prices and/or making incremental quality enhancements to capture market share.

While there are other possibilities, these are the tactics most often cited as typical of the competitive strategies pursued by many large Japanese companies.

To summarise, the strong competitiveness of Japanese companies in the open international market was largely attributable to low capital costs. Indeed many of the characteristics of so-called Japanese-style management – such as its emphasis on high quality, low prices and incremental improvements in products and technology, its long-term and aggressive approach to investment in plant and equipment, and 'lifetime' employment – were possible because Japanese firms enjoy a significant advantage when it comes to the cost of capital.

What made the Japanese approach even more powerful is its tolerance of low profitability, or even loss, for a sustained period of time if there was a consensus within the system that the investment has a strategic importance. Table 10.3, which compares the average returns on direct investment in Japan and the United States by large Japanese and US manufacturing companies during the 1980s, provides good evidence of the differences between the two systems. There was a consensus within Japan that maintaining or expanding market share in the United States through direct investment was so important that low profitability could be tolerated. In sharp contrast to Japanese manufacturers, who on average were barely breaking even on their US investments, US manufacturers were gaining a return of over 20 per cent on their Japanese operations.

Table 5.4, which provides annual data on the profitability of large Japanese and US corporations during the 1970s and 1980s, also confirms Japan's advantage. Japanese

TABLE 10.4 Profitability of foreign direct investment (per cent)

	Japanese investment in the US		*US investment in Japan*	
	Manufacturing	*Total*	*Manufacturing*	*Total*
1980	2.7	14.4	13.5	13.4
1985	–7.6	8.9	21.4	17.5
1986	–6.0	3.8	34.2	29.5
1987	3.9	3.5	27.9	25.5
1988	–0.5	3.3	19.9	21.0

Note: Profitability is defined as net profit for the period divided by average capital during the period.

Source: *Survey of Current Business*, US Department of Commerce, as cited by Masayuki Hara in 'US Direct Investment in Japan', *Journal of Japanese Trade and Industry*, no. 6 (MITI, 1990).

profitability, whether in terms of operating margin or return on equity, continued to decline during these two decades, when Japan was 'winning' against the United States in the international marketplace. In contrast, 'losing' US companies sustained or even improved their profitability during the same period.

It is often claimed that Japanese companies have adopted a low-return strategy in the short run with the long-run goal of driving out competitors, securing market dominance and reaping high profitability. Tables 10.4 and 5.4 indicate that this has not been the case. Historically, the profitability of Japanese companies has not increased even after they expanded their market share. Rather they have forced competitors to accept the low Japanese profitability standard. US companies have been unable to meet this challenge because the US financial system does not support such a low-return strategy. In the United States such a strategy would be met by a lower stock price, a reduced bond rating and a loss of competent managers. Before long any sensible US company would retreat from areas where the low return strategy proliferates, and redeploy capital and other resources into businesses where they could expect higher returns.

As a result Japanese companies have almost always turned out to be survivors in the markets they targeted. From that point of view, Japanese competition based on low-cost capital has been a very effective – though not necessarily efficient – approach in the open market system.

The above analysis applies to the entire large-company sector in Japan and the United States, but Japan's unique characteristic of 'high valuation of low profitability' seems also to apply to many individual cases. Table 10.5 compares the key financial indicators and PER of several pairs of well-managed Japanese and US companies belonging to similar industries in 1991. Except for the Ito Yokado/Walmart Stores pair, where the United States enjoyed both a higher profitability and a higher valuation, and the Nintendo/Apple pair, where Japan enjoyed a higher profitability and a higher valuation, the Japanese companies were given higher PERS even though their profitability was lower than that of their US counterparts.

10.4 CORPORATE PROFITABILITY AND CORPORATE GROWTH

The next question is how to reconcile the low-profitability strategy of Japanese companies with the phenomenally high growth of the Japanese economy for such a long time. As described in Chapter 3, low ROE means low growth of each unit of equity capital put into the value-creation process. If the aggregate value-creation activities of individual companies are somehow related to the value-creation activities of the entire economy, conventional wisdom tells us that low profitability tends to lead to lower growth of the economy rather than higher growth. This contradiction between the poor micro (company) financial performance and the excellent macro performance of Japan as a nation was possible because the main banks and other relationship shareholders

TABLE 10.5 Profitability and PER of selected pairs of Japanese and US companies

Company	*Revenue ($ mill)*	*Net income ($ mill)*	*Profit margin (%)*	*ROE (%)*	*Dividend yield (%)*	*PER*
Ito Yokado	13 248	501	3.8	15.4	0.5	26
Walmart Stores	32 602	1291	4.0	25.3	0.4	36
Hitachi	56 012	1665	3.0	8.2	0.9	17
General Electric	58 400	4300	7.4	19.9	2.6	16
Fujitsu	21 501	599	2.8	7.6	0.8	25
IBM	69 000	6020	8.7	12.8	4.6	11
Nintendo	3410	499	14.6	36.3	0.3	29
Apple Computer	5558	475	8.5	32.9	1.0	11
NTT	45 247	1709	3.8	5.9	0.5	60
AT&T	37 300	2740	7.3	19.7	3.6	15
Kao	4793	145	3.0	7.7	0.6	35
P&G	24 081	1602	6.7	22.4	2.3	17
Mitsubishi Trust	–	298	–	5.1	0.4	62
J. P. Morgan	–	775	–	17.9	3.6	12
Canon	12 510	445	3.6	9.9	0.8	18
Hewlett-Packard	13 233	739	5.6	12.7	0.9	16

Source: Compiled from 'The Global 1000', *Business Week*, 15 July 1991.

were willing to support the physical expansion of their client companies even though their marginal profitability continued to decline over time.

Imagine a situation in which a major Japanese car manufacturer decides to make a massive investment in a new manufacturing plant in North America in order to overcome protectionist measures against imported cars. The project is of such a scale that the company needs to double both its debt and its shareholders' equity. The new plant is expected to reach full-scale production soon after its completion because the company is determined to sell high-quality cars at a relatively low price compared with its US and European competitors in the North American market. The marginal ROE for the expansion will be, say, 6 per cent, compared with the current ROE of 10 per cent. As a result the average ROE of this company after its major new investment will fall from 10 per cent to 8 per cent. Will and should relationship shareholders such as a main bank and a major trading firm belonging to the same business group support this project and provide financing? The main bank will benefit from expanding long-term and short-term lending to this important client. It will also be asked to handle all the foreign exchange transactions arising from the project, as well the local financing requirements through its North American subsidiary. Therefore the main bank is very likely to support the project and provide both debt and equity financing even though the marginal ROE may fall. Likewise the trading firm will also regard this as a very attractive project and worthy of support.

Hence this major new investment project will be fully supported by the principal lenders and shareholders even though they know that marginal profitability will be much lower than the current average. For them the benefits arising from the expansion of the client company's business will outweigh the marginal decline in ROE.

The same logic can be applied to any new investment projects by major Japanese companies. These new investments will of course lead to an increase in production and employment, and ultimately in higher GNP growth. Increases in macro indicators such as industrial production level and GNP do not necessarily go hand-in-hand with a high return on shareholders' capital. When international competition is an important part of macro growth, lower profitability may be more consistent with high GNP growth. From this point of view, giving a high valuation to a company that showed a high growth in size was consistent with the economic goals of Japan even if its profitability was low and continued to decline over time.

An economy that is attuned to low profitability will of course tend to have a high investment rate. In addition, growth in the size of an operation will also bring about an important competitive advantage if economies of scale and the learning curve are at work in that industry. For this reason, Japan's choice of the 'better and cheaper' strategy was a very powerful one and the financial system was a key underpinning factor.

11 International Comparison of the Cost of Capital

11.1 THE COST-OF-CAPITAL CONCEPT

Required corporate profitability measured by traditional financial accounting numbers is, so to speak, a historical average cost of capital or required return on capital. If the Japanese financial system tolerated low corporate profitability and valued it highly in the credit and stock market, the logical consequence is that the cost of capital implicit in the current market price would have been very low for Japanese companies compared with their US and European competitors. This chapter focuses on a comparison of the market-based cost of capital of major nations.

The market cost of capital conceptually corresponds to the expected return for investors implicit in the current market price of debt securities and shares. In the case of debt, it corresponds to the effective interest rate. In the case of stock it corresponds to the discount factor, which equates the discounted present value of expected future dividends to the current share price, assuming the share is efficiently priced. Company managers are expected to use the same rates weighted by the debt and equity mix of the company as the hurdle rate when they discount expected cash flows for their new investment opportunities.

Estimating an effective interest rate is not a difficult problem. For example the effective cost (before tax) of long-term debt capital can be estimated by computing the yield to maturity of an appropriate long-term corporate bond.

Estimating the cost of equity is more difficult, and several different approaches have been used. One approach is to start with the current per-share earnings yield (after-tax, per-share income divided by the current share price, or the reverse of PER), and to make depreciation and other necessary adjustments to reported income so that it reflects a truly sustainable economic income rather than accounting income. This approach assumes that in the long run the ROE, or current after-tax earnings per share divided by the current share price, will become equal to expected return or the cost of equity capital. Another approach involves estimating investors' total expected return on stocks by adding the expected dividend yield and the expected growth in earnings or dividends per share, using consensus forecasts by professional security analysts. McCauley and Zimmer's study, which is summarised in the following section, used the former approach and Malkiel used the latter.

For an international comparison of the market cost of capital, further adjustments become necessary to allow for the difference among nations in inflation rates, tax rates, accounting treatments of inventory valuation and depreciation, corporate liquidity requirements, the effects of cross-holding shares and the degree of consolidation of financial reporting.

11.2 EMPIRICAL FINDINGS

A most comprehensive and detailed study of the market cost of capital among major nations was conducted by McCauley and Zimmer of the Federal Reserve Bank of New York.[1] They estimated and compared the cost of debt and equity for the United States, Japan, Britain and Germany during the 1980s based on the first of the two approaches described in the previous section.

They defined the cost of debt as the real (after adjustment for inflation) after-tax interest rate for corporate borrowers.

They started with a weighted average of rates on bank and bond debt adjusted for the differing propensities of firms to hold liquid assets. Then they subtracted the actual inflation rate to produce a standard real rate of interest. Finally they corrected for allowable tax deductions on corporate interest payments in order to place costs on a real after-tax basis. The results are shown on the left-hand side of Figure 11.1. They discovered that during a large part of the 1980s there was not a significant difference in the real, after-tax cost of debt among the United States, Britain and Japan. Germany enjoyed the lowest cost of debt, largely because of its heavy reliance on bank debt.

To estimate the cost of equity, they started with the inverse of PER that the equity market assigned to a given stream of earnings. Then they made various adjustments to reported earnings to produce a true cost of equity. Some adjustments were made for all countries for the effects of inflation on depreciation, on inventory profits and on nominal interest payments, and for the different prospects of growth in corporate earnings. Other adjustments were country-specific – for Japan, an adjustment for the cross-holding of shares; for Japan and Germany, adjustments stemming from additions to reserves for employees' retirement payments. After making all these adjustments, they obtained the cost of equity in the four nations shown in Figure 11.1. In general, Japanese companies enjoyed lower equity costs than the other three nations, and US companies generally faced the highest equity costs. The effect of bull stock markets in the 1980s was evident in a generally declining trend for equity costs in all four nations.

A comparison of debt and equity costs showed that debt was generally cheaper than equity. Only for Japan in the latter half of the 1980s were the two costs identical. This finding seems to confirm my argument that in Japan the risk premium on equity, if any, was negligible.

Then they combined the costs of debt and equity, weighted by book debt and market equity, to produce a weighted-average, after-tax cost of capital, or 'cost of funds' in their terminology. Japan and Germany enjoyed significantly lower

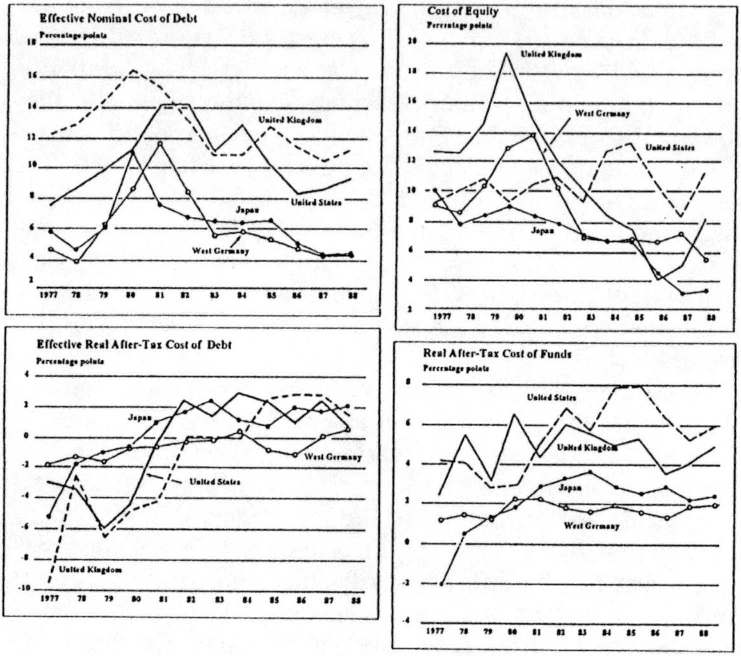

Source: *Shoken Analysts Journal* (*Security Analysts Journal*), March 1992.

FIGURE 11.1 International comparison of cost of capital: estimates by the Federal Reserve Bank of New York, 1977–88

average costs of capital. Compared with the United States and Britain, Japan's advantage derived from cheap debt and equity while Germany's advantage came from cheap debt.

Malkiel estimated and compared the cost of equity using a totally different approach[2] based on survey data that reflected the actual expectations of equity investors. His approach assumed that the valuation of common stocks was based on the constant growth version of the dividend discount model, as introduced in Chapter 3. The equity investors' expected return, k_e, or the cost of equity for borrowing companies, can be expressed as:

$$k_e = (D_o[1+g]/P_o)+g$$

Using this model, we can estimate the cost of equity by estimating (1) the current dividend yield and (2) the expected long-term growth rate of dividend per share. Dividends and share price data are readily available for the market as a whole, and long-term (five-year) growth rate forecasts can be obtained from a variety of forecasters, including financial service firms. Malkiel put together such information and produced estimates of the cost of equity in the United States, Germany and Japan, both nominal and real, for 1977–89. The results are shown in Table 11.1a. In spite of the different methodologies used, the results of the Malkiel and the McCauley–Zimmer studies were surprisingly similar, as shown in Table 11.1b. Other studies, including those by James Poterba[3] and Frankel,[4] also came to the conclusion that Japanese companies enjoyed lower cost of capital throughout most of the late 1970s and 1980s.

If the main banks are to support the low return strategy of the Japanese manufacturing sector, the cost of capital for banks also has to be low. In other words, to complete the full circle the system has to be able to tolerate a low level of profitability among both companies and large banks. We should not be surprised, then, to find that a common strategy of major Japanese banks has been to sacrifice profitability for growth in size. The banks' average pretax return on assets in recent years has been about half, or less than half, that of the leading US and British banks.[5] The major Japanese banks were able to dominate the international leading market in the 1980s basically by providing high-quality capital with low lending rates, largely because the system tolerated low returns while encouraging growth in size. It should also be noted that Japanese banks, like Japan's non-financial sector, had one of the lowest equity cushions among industrialised countries.

TABLE 11.1 International comparison of cost of capital: estimates by Malkiel

(a) Estimates of the cost of equity capital: $k_e = (D_0[1 + g]/P_0) + g$

	Nominal (%)			*Real (%)*		
	US	*Japan*	*Germany*	*US*	*Japan*	*Germany*
1977	11.4	11.4	10.2	6.2	6.5	6.3
1978	14.9	10.3	9.6	6.8	6.1	5.9
1979	14.4	9.7	9.4	6.7	6.0	5.9
1980	13.4	9.1	9.2	7.7	6.3	6.0
1981	13.3	7.9	8.8	8.0	5.7	6.0
1982	13.7	7.2	8.7	9.4	5.6	6.4
1983	11.9	7.1	7.5	7.9	5.6	5.4
1984	12.1	6.8	7.1	8.3	5.5	5.2
1985	10.9	6.3	6.8	7.3	5.0	4.9
1986	10.0	6.2	6.3	6.2	4.7	4.2
1987	9.8	6.5	7.1	5.6	4.8	4.7
1988	10.5	6.7	7.8	6.3	5.0	5.2
1989	10.3	6.3	7.8	5.9	4.8	4.6
Average 1980–89	11.6	7.0	7.7	7.3	5.3	5.5

(b) Comparison of the two estimates (average 1980–88, %)

	US	*Japan*	*Germany*
k_e (Malkiel estimate)	11.7	7.1	7.7
k_e (McCauley–Zimmer estimate)	10.6	6.0	8.3

Sources: Burton G. Malkiel, 'The Concept and International Comparison of the Cost of Capital', *Shoken Analysts Journal* (*Security Analysts Journal*) March 1992.

The international competitiveness of large Japanese banks during the 1980s, as measured by the cost of capital, can be illustrated more dramatically by measuring the cost of their equity capital implicit in the stock price. As shown in Figure 11.2, McCauley and Zimmer discovered that, among industrialised nations, Japan's advantage in the cost of equity capital was even more conspicuous for banks than for non-financial companies.[6] This is consistent with the fact that large banks have been at the heart of Japan's relationship-based financial and business system, and that their shares are among

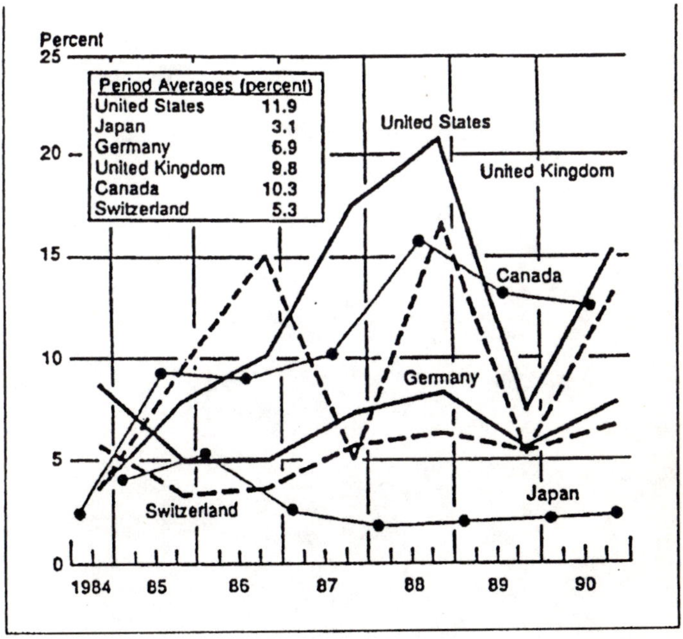

Source: *Shoken Analysts Journal* (*Security Analysts Journal*) March 1992.

FIGURE 11.2 Cost of banks' equity capital

the most heavily cross-held.[7] According to the Fair Trade Commission,[8] the main banks have cross-holding arrangements with virtually all member companies of the Mitsui, Mitsubishi and Sumitomo groups.

Part IV

Critical Reassessment of Japanese Capitalism as a Catch-up Model

12 Japan's National Value-Creation Process

12.1 THE ROLE OF COMPANIES

In assessing the merits and demerits of Japanese capitalism we must first address the issue of management objectives and constraints. In other words, what are the primary roles of companies in the nation's economy, what are they expected to maximise and how are they expected to contribute to the nation's economic goals? Unless we specify the objectives of management we cannot evaluate their performance.

In US capitalism, each investor-owned company is expected to be an independent and self-contained micro unit of resource allocation decisions whose performance is ultimately evaluated by the productivity of shareholders' capital, or ROE. That is not exactly the case with Japanese capitalism. In contrast to US capitalism, in which value creation depends on the initiative of individuals, investors and company managers, the Japanese value-creation process starts with the managers and administrators of the nation, and companies and individuals are expected to contribute in the most effective manner possible to achieve the nation's current economic goals. Since continued high growth of the economy, or GNP, has been the primary and everlasting economic goal of the nation, large Japanese companies have been strongly encouraged to contribute to the maximum growth possibilities of, say, production, exports, employment or physical investment in plant and equipment, even at the cost of efficiency and profitability. As a result, large US companies and large Japanese companies could well have competed under a different set of objectives and constraints. Table 12.1 compares and contrast' the US and Japanese environments.

As described in Part I, there is a strong consensus in the central marketplace that investor-owned companies should maximise the return on their shareholders' capital. This does not mean that the management of companies cares only about shareholders' wealth. On the contrary, managers of large companies are increasingly under pressure to care about all stakeholders, including employees, suppliers, local communities, the government and the environment. However these constraints are shared by all competitors and all companies are forced to compete for the most efficient use of economic and managerial resources, which is ultimately measured by the productivity of shareholders' capital.

In contrast the primary objective of large investor-owned Japanese companies was not to maximise the return on their shareholders' capital. Rather there was a much greater focus on achieving maximum growth of physical measures such as production, exports or employment. As a means of contrasting Japanese capitalism with the US paradigm of maximising

TABLE 12.1 Management objectives and constraints contrasted: Japan vs the United States

	US: central marketplace	*Japan: local unit*
Objective	Maximise shareholders' wealth (ROE)	Maximise employment of Japanese workforce
Major constraints	Fair competition Welfare of employees Coprosperity with suppliers and subcontractors Contribution to local communities Good corporate citizenship, etc.	Scarce capital and hard currency Lack of basic technologies Lack of natural resources etc. Maximum access to open international market

ROE in terms of company objective, I will characterise that of Japanese management as maximising employment (of Japanis workforce). There has been a strong consensus in Japan until very recently that companies belong to their employees, even though they are legally owned by shareholders. Itami's naming of Japanese capitalism as 'peopleism' as opposed to 'investor capitalism' reflects this paradigm.[1] In Japanese capitalism, providing a return on shareholders' capital is regarded as one of many constraints; companies are only expected to achieve a sufficient return on shareholders' capital to pay the stable dividend, as described in Chapter 7.

As a small and isolated archipelago poorly endowed with natural resources, the only valuable economic resource Japan has had in abundance was its industrious and well-educated workforce. Therefore it was logical for those running Japan to insist that contribution to maximising employment of its workforce should be the primary objective of the management of large companies.

There has also been strong external support for Japan's objectives. The consensus firmly shared by the postwar Western allies was that Japan should emerge as a strong democratic and prosperous nation based on the principles of the capitalist free market economy. Consequently Japan was strongly encouraged to take a full advantage of the open international market to sell its manufactured goods and purchase natural resources, technology, ideas and know-how.

The importance to the economic success of Japan of the development of the open market for multilateral trade under the Bretton Woods regime cannot be overemphasised. As long as the international market for raw materials as well as basic and advanced technology is open to Japan, its economic growth will continue. But if for any reason it were to be shut out, as was the case immediately before and during the Second World War, it would have to fall back on its own resources and could not possibly feed its one hundred million people. Without the open market for manufactured products, Japan would never have become a leading economic nation producing 15 per cent of the world's GNP.

In order to make full use of the open international market for the nation's value creation, Japan had to accumulate dollars, the hard currency. Although Japan consistently and successfully pursued a high savings policy in the domestic economy, it was of no use in the international marketplace unless domestic savings could be converted into dollars (the yen was not widely accepted in the international marketplace until well into the 1970s). As a result Japan chose the manufacturing industries as the main dollar earners and supported them in their attempt to compete and survive in the international competition, first through cheap, high-quality labour and later through low-cost capital.

Under the macroeconomic objectives and constraints discussed above, Japanese companies were expected to contribute directly to nation's economic goals. In order to contribute to maximising the nation's employment, they single-mindedly pursued physical growth as if this were the prime management objective.

12.2 JAPAN'S ECONOMIC VALUE-CREATION PROCESS

If economic value-creation decisions have rested with the nation rather than individual companies in Japan, we must now address the primary objectives, constraints and strategies of Japan in its economic value-creation effort. Of course this is a very broad and controversial subject. Here I will address the subject primarily by extending the same value-creation framework for individual companies described in Part I to the nation of Japan as if it were a large single company. It is my contention that Japan's national strategy has not been very different from the US model in that it has also sought to maximise capital productivity. The difference, though, is that Japan has sought to maximise the input–output efficiency of the dollar in its economic activities through the open international market.

Since Japan has been strongly encouraged to prosper by fully utilising the open market, not just as an outlet for its products but also for procuring basic technology, ideas, management know-how, raw materials and capital goods, the scarcity of indigenous raw materials, lack of basic technology and the smallness of the domestic market have constituted relative rather than absolute obstacles to economic development.

The need to rely heavily on large manufacturing companies as the principal earners of hard currency for the nation seems to be the single most important factor that differentiates Japanese company management from US management. For US companies, earning dollars for the nation makes no sense. For all other nations, earning hard currency is one of the most important considerations in economic policy, for obvious reasons. To achieve this, many developed and developing nations are able to sell international commodities such as crude oil, iron ore, timber, cotton, sugar, coffee beans, beef and so on whose market prices are quoted daily in the open international marketplace. Farmers, miners or planters may or may not make a profit at the current prices, but nations can at least procure the dollars they need through the sale of these commodities in the international market.

For postwar Japan, which was endowed with nothing but its one hundred million people, the only way to earn dollars systematically was to mobilise this rich stock of human resources to add value to imported raw materials, technology and ideas, produce exportable manufactured products and earn more dollars than were put into the process.

Hence the formula for the economic development of Japan was strategically to allocate scarce capital, and especially foreign reserves, so that Japanese exporting companies could survive and expand in the open international market and thus earn more dollars, which could then be reinvested to fuel further economic growth, leading to the maximisation of employment of Japan's workforce.

There was no reason for Japanese companies not to seek higher returns. However the Japanese system clearly favoured and rewarded them handsomely if they earned more dollars through increased exports by sacrificing some part of profitability. The reward came in the form of a favourable allocation of capital and other resources that would enable expansion, as well as a high valuation in the credit and capital market. Since these dollar earners were the primary borrowers in the credit and capital market, they naturally came to set the standard for acceptable minimum profitability for the entire system.

As a consequence earning as many dollars as possible was of very high priority, certainly much higher than achieving a high ROE, for the managers of many large Japanese manufacturing companies. Figure 12.1 shows the national version of the economic value-creation framework introduced in Part I.

Like a company, Japan carefully allocated scarce dollars to important industries, companies or projects to purchase from the international marketplace whatever was needed to start the economic value-creation process. In fact the influence that the Ministry of Trade and Industry International (MITI) was able to exert over Japanese industries came from its authority to allocate dollars during the reconstruction and high growth era. Since Japan lacked most of the raw materials used by its industries, a large part of the dollar reserves were used to import natural resources. Another priority in the early years was to import basic and advanced technologies, mostly from advanced industrialised nations, so that Japan could focus on the improvement and application of these technologies.

Japan put these resources into what I call the Japanese management system. This system comprised many elements, including a homogeneous society, stable political system, strong government initiatives and interventions based on cordial government and business relations, a well-educated and well-disciplined workforce, the relationship-based business system, the lifetime employment system and company labour unions, *keiretsu* or business groupings, the high-saving culture, egalitarian values and so on. It mobilised the Japanese citizenry primarily through the companies, many of which belonged to established business groups. The well-educated,

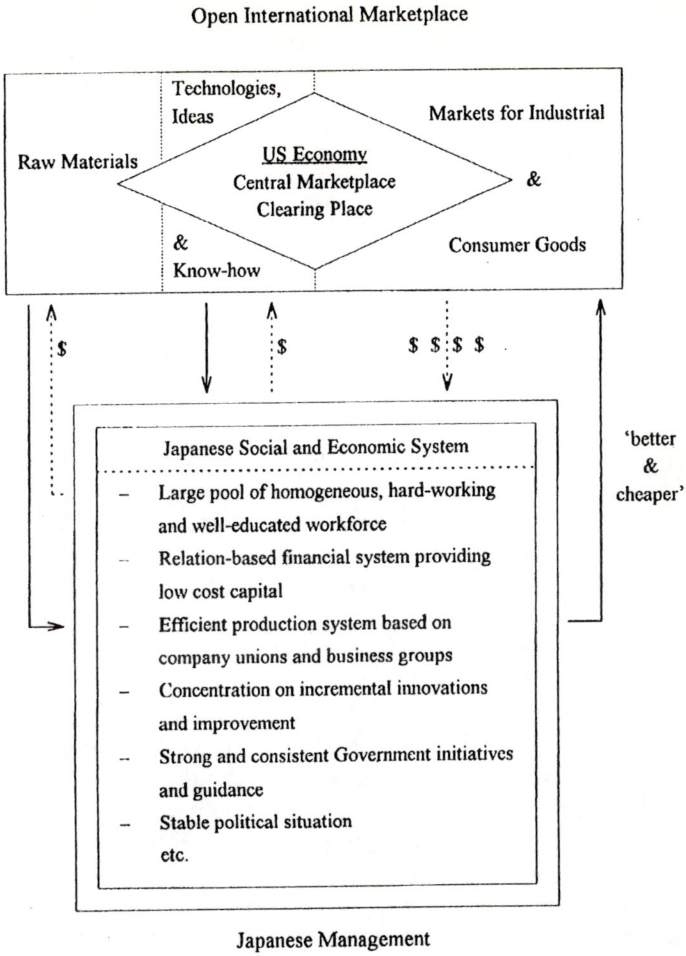

FIGURE 12.1 Japan's traditional value creation process

well-disciplined Japanese workforce added value in the value-creation process, mass produced high-quality products and delivered them at a very competitive price to the international marketplace to recover as many dollars as possible. Until the early 1970s all the dollars earned by Japanese exporters had to be handed over to the Bank of Japan. They were then plowed back into the value-creation process, again after careful judgement as to their allocation. If Japan could perpetuate this value-creation process through the international market, its economy could keep growing without limit. Therefore Japan's primary objective in its value-creation process could be defined as maximising, return on the dollar, or maximisation of the output to input ratio of dollars just as individual companies try to do with shareholders' capital in the US model.

A key factor of success in this process was the fact that Japan's industrial and engineering capability was sufficient to allow it to integrate basic and advanced imported technology into its value-creation process by improving it, often through reverse engineering, and applying it to various commercial and productive processes, leading to the mass production of high-quality manufactured goods at a very competitive price for export. From the very early years Japan was able compete with the technologically elite members of the world industrial league: the United States, Germany, Britain and a few others. All these competitors were high-wage nations compared with Japan until the early 1970s when Japan used up its cheap-labour advantage.

In this process, it is obvious that the lower the minimum required profitability, or return on shareholders' capital, the easier it was for Japan to deliver better and cheaper products, leading to more dollars for the nation. For this reason Japan's low-profitability strategy was exactly suited to its objective of maximising dollar earnings. This is why ROE was made a constraint rather than an objective to be maximised in Japanese capitalism. The return on shareholders' capital could be minimised by setting a stable dividend as if it were an interest charge on debt capital.

13 The Merits and Demerits of Japanese Capitalism

13.1 JAPAN'S EXCELLENT MACRO PERFORMANCE

By any conventional measures, Japan's economic value-creation process has been extraordinarily successful. It has achieved long-term, sustained and stable high growth under moderate to low inflation, and the fruits of economic development and prosperity have been widely shared by its citizens. In fact Japan has become one of the world's richest and most egalitarian societies in terms of distribution of income and economic welfare, and is sometimes referred to as the most successful socialist economy.

By the early 1980s Japan had emerged as the second largest economy in the world, and by the mid 1980s it had become the world's largest creditor nation due to its sustained large balance-of-payments surplus. It has also heavily influenced the phenomenal economic growth of many other nations in North-East and South-East Asia and has come to be regarded as the leader of the group of 'developmental capitalist' states.

The World Bank recently published a report analysing the phenomenal macroeconomic performance of eight East Asian economies led by Japan.[1] The eight economies include Japan, the 'Four Tigers' (Hong Kong, the Republic of Korea, Singapore and Taiwan, China) and the three newly industrialising economies of South-East Asia: Indonesia, Malaysia and Thailand. The World Bank called these economies the eight high-performing Asian economies (HPAEs) and analysed the common factors behind their success.

A comparison of the long-term economic performance (1960–85) of many nations was made using two of the most important macroeconomics indicators, that is, average real GDP growth per capita and income equality in the society. The results are shown in Figure 13.1. It was found that the the best-performer category was monopolised by seven of the eight HPAEs (upper left-hand corner of Figure 13.1). According to the World Bank the probability of seven economies from the same region monopolising the highest growth group would be one in ten thousand if the growth had taken place randomly. Since the excellent performance of the HPAEs seemed to be more than just a coincidence, they tried to identify some common features of these economies in the areas of economic, industrial and social policy. Following is the list of the common features they identified, and they claim that many of these were first developed by Japan.

1. Public policies and growth:
   - market-friendly view;
   - a functional approach to understanding growth.
2. Achieving macroeconomic stability and export growth.
3. Building the institutional basis for growth:
   - adhering to the principle of shared growth;
   - creating a business-friendly environment;
   - use of deliberation council.
4. Accumulating human and physical capital:
   - building human capital;
   - increasing savings and investment.
5. Efficient allocation and productivity change:
   - flexible labour market;
   - capital market and allocation;
   - openness to foreign technology;
   - promoting specific industries;
   - export push: a winning mix of fundamentals and intervention.

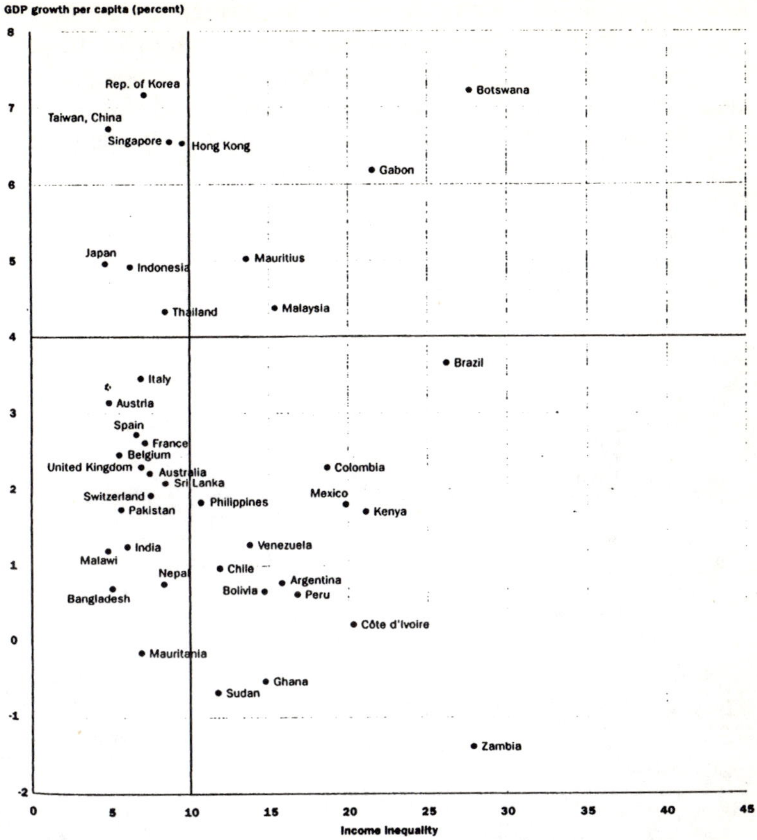

Note: Income inequality is measured by the ratio of the income shares of the richest 20 per cent and the poorest 20 per cent of the population.

Source: *The East Asian Miracle*, World Bank Policy Research Report (Oxford University Press, 1993), p. 31.

FIGURE 13.1 Macroeconomic performance of selected nations, 1960–85

Another aspect of Japan's economic performance that might also suggest that Japanese capitalism is a somewhat better model than others is the extreme stability that accompanied the high growth. Figure 13.2 provides evidence of this stability. The deviation each year of real GNP growth from the

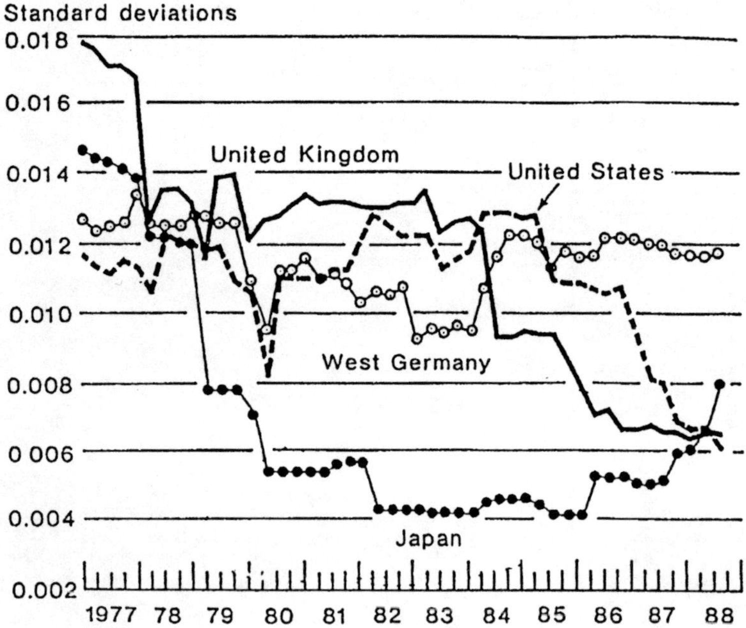

Note: Data are moving five-year standard deviations of percentage changes in the gross national product.

Source: Developed by Robert N. McCauley and Steven A. Zimmer, based on the following sources: UK Central Statistical Office, US Department of Commerce, International Monetary Fund, *Shoken Analysts Journal* (*Security Analysts Journal*), March 1992.

FIGURE 13.2 Volatility of real GNP, 1977–88

average was significantly smaller for Japan than for other major industrial nations from 1977–88, except in 1978–79 when the oil price surged due to the second oil crisis. Figure 13.3 provides further evidence, this time at the industrial level. The number of cars produced by the Japanese automobile industry increased very steadily from 1959–89 as if it had been planned, while that for the United States fluctuated widely. Of course this was a direct consequence of the 'better and cheaper' strategy of the Japanese companies to increase their international market share, especially in the North American market, no matter how much fluctuation there might be in the aggregate demand for cars. Compared with the Japanese automobile companies, the US 'Big Three' had to accommodate themselves to the full fluctuation of the aggregate demand minus whatever proportion the Japanese took of it.

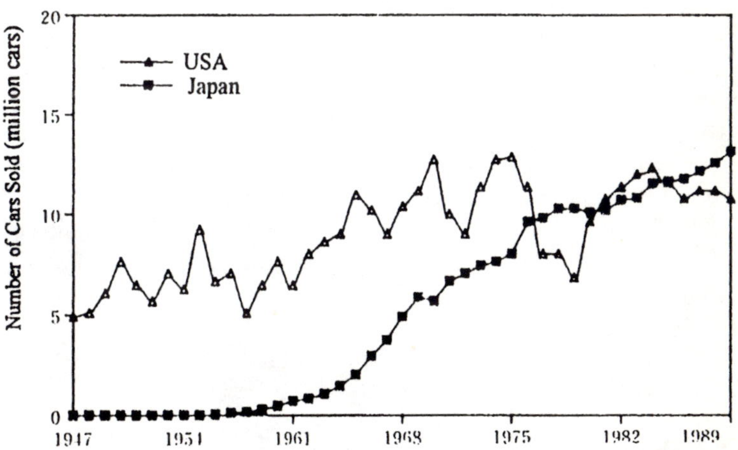

Source: D. Roos *et al.*, *The Machine that Changed the World* (London: Macmillan, 1990).

FIGURE 13.3 Growth of the automobile industry, 1947–89

Japan's achievement in the areas of capital accumulation and human resource utilisation have also been very impressive. Table 13.1 shows that by the early 1980s Japan had achieved its long-term objective of fully employing the Japanese workforce, while at the same time ridding itself of the long-term constraint imposed by the dollar shortage.

By 1980 the Japanese balance of payments had become a solid surplus, and as the 1980s evolved the surplus continued to accumulate rapidly. As a result, Japan's official foreign reserves soared even after the holding of foreign reserves and foreign investment by the private sector was gradually liberalised. By the mid 1980s Japan had become the largest net creditor nation, replacing the United States, and the need to allocate 'scarce' dollars finally vanished. Reflecting the huge current account surplus, the financial assets of Japan's household sector also increased markedly during the 1980s and the household saving rate continued at a relatively high level. Probably the most important evidence of Japan's enormous economic success is the marked improvement in the living standard of Japanese citizens, shown above all in the ever-rising average life expectancy. Today, on average Japanese people live for eighty years, the longest among the major nations of the world. When Japan began its economic development programme after the Second World War the average life expectancy was merely a little over 60 years.

Much more has been written and said about the positive side of Japanese economic development, and therefore I shall call a halt at this point.

13.2 LIMITATIONS AND WEAKNESSES

There have been lot of arguments for and against the Japanese government's heavy 'hands-on' approach to economic development, especially from the viewpoint of whether it could provide a better or more effective model, than the US or neoclassical open market model for developing nations with severe resource constraints.

TABLE 13.1 Japan's performance: financial and human resources, 1981–93

	1981	*1982*	*1983*	*1984*	*1985*	*1986*	*1987*	*1988*	*1989*	*1990*	*1991*	*1992*	*1993*
GNP growth (real, %)*	3.2	3.5	3.0	4.4	4.6	2.9	4.7	6.0	4.3	5.3	3.6	0.4	0.0
Current account surplus ($ bill.)*	4.8	6.9	20.8	35.0	49.2	85.8	87.0	79.6	57.2	33.7	90.2	125.9	130.5
Official reserves ($ bill.)*	28.4	23.3	24.5	26.3	26.5	42.2	81.5	97.7	84.9	69.9	68.2	70.0	101.7
Net external credit ($ bill.)*	10.9	24.7	37.3	74.3	129.8	180.4	240.7	291.7	293.2	328.1	383.1	513.6	610.8
Yen-dollar rate (yen)	220	235	232	252	201	160	122	126	143	135	125	125	112
Household financial assets (trillion yen)*	390	436	492	538	594	663	733	814	898	955	985	1025	1075
Ditto, times of Current GNP*	1.4	1.5	1.7	1.7	1.8	2.0	2.1	2.1	2.3	2.4	2.4	2.4	2.3
Pensions asset (trillion yen)*	9.7	11.7	14.0	16.6	19.5	22.7	26.3	30.0	34.4	38.6	42.9	47.2	51.5
Population growth (%)	0.7	0.7	0.7	0.6	0.7	0.5	0.5	0.4	0.4	0.3	0.3	0.3	0.3
Labour force growth (%)	1.0	1.1	1.3	1.2	1.3	1.3	1.4	1.3	1.3	1.2	1.1	1.1	0.6
Unemployment (%)	2.2	2.4	2.6	2.7	2.6	2.8	2.8	2.5	2.3	2.1	2.1	2.2	2.5
Job vacancy/application	0.7	0.6	0.6	0.7	0.7	0.6	0.7	1.0	1.3	1.4	1.4	1.1	0.8
Population aged over 65 (%)	9.3	9.6	9.8	9.9	10.2	10.5	10.8	11.2	11.5	12.0	12.5	13.1	13.5
Birth rate (per 1000)	13.0	12.8	12.7	12.5	11.9	11.4	11.1	10.8	10.2	9.9	9.9	9.8	9.6
Reproduction rate per woman	1.7	1.8	1.8	1.8	1.8	1.7	1.7	1.7	1.6	1.5	1.5	1.5	1.5

Note: Items with an asterisk are for fiscal years; all others are for calendar years.

Sources: Various governmental and industrial sources.

Adherents to the neoclassical view stress that the approach of Japan and the other HPAEs can be placed within the neoclassical framework, and that their success lies in getting the basics right according to market economic theory.

Adherents to the 'revisionist' view claim that some of the policies of Japan and the other HPAEs have been much more in accord with models of state-led development and that these governments deliberately 'got the prices wrong' (altering the incentive structure) to boost industries that would not otherwise have thrived.[2]

Instead of embroiling myself in this controversy, I would like to discuss the limitations and problems of the Japanese approach as a resource allocation model.

3.2.1 Local Optimisation and Temporary Objectives

A major success of Japanese capitalism is the fact that Japan achieved its long-term national objective of maximising employment while at the same time overcoming the long-term constraint imposed by the dollar shortage. However these achievements also marked the beginning of many new problems and challenges. Seen as a resource allocation system, the biggest challenge has been to change the traditional combination of objective and constraint, that is, achieving maximum employment through the strategic allocation of scarce dollars. In other words, unlike the universal US approach of allocating economic resources largely through the open market system, Japan's approach sought a local optimisation conditional on the openness of the international market system. Even though it lasted over 40 years, the objective – constraint combination was essentially temporary. It and the allocation process had to be constantly and carefully monitored and fine-tuned in response to the degree of success achieved. With each step forward the managers of the system were required to exercise even more and better judgment. There was a need to create greater consensus and introduce even more careful planning and control. Otherwise resources could be misallocated and could create frictions and conflict with the central marketplace. The system might also have become vulnerable to corruption and social injustice, just as in the case of many centrally planned economies. We will deal with some of these issues in Chapter 14.

13.2.2 The Self-Defeating Zero-Sum Game

I have pointed out the similarities in the value-creation frameworks of the US and Japanese models, but there is one important difference: the US model for private companies is expected to lead to a big 'plus-sum' game. All commercially oriented companies operate with an eye to profit and all company managers are expected to maximise the profits on the capital put in their hands.

The Japanese national strategy of maximising dollar productivity, if successful, will lead to Japan becoming a winner in an essentially 'zero-sum' game. To the extent that Japan would win a surplus in this game, the rest of the world, by definition, must lose by the same amount. Under the current international monetary system, if Japan keeps winning the game there will inevitably be pressure to push up the exchange rate of the yen versus all other foreign currencies, including the US dollar. In other words, Japan's 'better and cheaper' approach will sooner or later result in the country losing its international competitiveness, thus becoming a victim of its own success. It is essentially a self-defeating game.

13.2.3 Disequilibriating Protectionism

Unlike many other developed and developing nations, Japan tried to maximise production and export regardless of their ability to consume and import. As a consequence, Japan's continued success created a huge and increasing disequilibrium in the global economic system. In fact, the 'market-friendly' view taken by Japan was the one friendly to the open external market place; her domestic market had been heavily controlled and protected against and closed to foreigners. This was, of course, consistent with Japan's traditional strategy but reinforced and prolonged the disequilibrium until it accelerated the upward revaluation of yen to an unsustainable level of $1 = ¥80 in the middle of 1995. It was this high yen which finally forced many large Japanese manufacturers to relocate their plants in other parts of the world and to ship their products back to their home market, importing into the heavily protected market for the first time in the history of Japan.

13.2.4 Accommodation of Low Efficiency

Another serious problem with Japanese capitalism is the fact that it tends to accommodate or tolerate low efficiency and low productivity as a result of encouraging low profitability. In contrast with the US, which forces all companies to compete for operational efficiency and high profitability, Japanese capitalism has emphasised coexistence, harmony and the sharing of fruits among all Japanese citizens. As part of this long-term package deal, Japanese citizens have been willing to tolerate many things, including low interest rates on bank deposits, low ROE, long working-hours, rising land prices and so on.

Throughout this book I have emphasised the low productivity of capital in Japan. If a low return on shareholders' capital has been tolerated and even supported, the same should be true of, say, the productivity of labour. And indeed this has been the case.

Table 13.2 compares the total working hours of employees in the manufacturing sector of several nations. In 1990 Japanese employees worked 2120 hours each, which was by far the largest among industralised nations. Compared with Germany, which also achieved phenomenal economic success after the Second World War, Japanese workers on average spent 30 per cent more time in the workplace. This comparison suggests that Japan put in a lot more man-hours than Germany for a similar macroeconomic achievement.

Table 13.3 provides a more precise comparison of labour productivity in four countries (the United States, Germany, France and Britain), with Japan acting as the benchmark at

TABLE 13.2 International comparison of annual work hours (manufacturing sector)

	Japan	*US*	*Britain*	*Germany*	*France*	*Korea*
1982	2140	1841	1844	1684	1700	2792
1983	2152	1908	1848	1698	1683	2829
1984	2178	1934	1876	1701	1679	2824
1985	2166	1929	1890	1682	1671	2798
1986	2150	1929	1890	1667	1675	2844
1987	2161	1940	1894	1643	1675	2808
1988	2180	1960	1913	1645	1684	2735
1989	2155	1950	1917	1632	1679	2636
1990	2120	1940	1912	1613	1679	2590
1991	2076	1934	1863	n.a.	1666	n.a.

Source: Comparative economic and financial statistics, Japan and other major nations (Tokyo, Bank of Japan, 1992)

100. If we use the exchange rates prevailing in the year of reference, Japan ranked number one in terms of average labour productivity for all industries, and the Japanese manufacturing sector led those of the other nations by a wide margin. But if we use exchange rates based on purchasing power parity, we get an entirely different picture. Japan was least productive in the all-industry average and its manufacturing sector ranked third, far behind that of the United States. Thus even manufacturing, the most productive and competitive part of the Japanese economy, was not that productive in terms of labour input and output. The agricultural and distribution sectors performed very poorly in this comparison.

It is widely believed that the Japanese manufacturing companies, especially those competing in the export market, are very efficient, productive and competitive. How can we reconcile the statistics in Tables 13.2 and 13.3 with this generally accepted belief? Referring back to Table 10.5 may provide some insight into this.

TABLE 13.3 International comparison of labour productivity (Japan = 100)

	Japan	US (1989)		Germany (1988)		France (1989)		Britain (1987)	
		Market exchange rate	*Purchasing parity rate*	*Market exchange rate*	*Purchasing parity rate*	*Market exchange rate*	*Purchasing parity rate*	*Market exchange rate*	*Purchasing parity rate*
Average productivity for	100	95	141	93	108	95	120	68	105
all industries(per hour)	100	109	162	119	139	116	146	n/a	n/a
Manufacturing industries	100	80	118	77	90	80	101	52	81
(per hour)	100	88	130	103	120	105	132	58	90
Agriculture and other primary industries	100	212	313	95	111	153	194	123	189
Distribution industries	100	129	190	107	125	153	193	71	109
Conversion rate (yen per US dollar)		137.96	204	72.98	85.25	21.62	27.31	236.34	364.57

Source: Ministry of Labour, as reported in *Nihon Keizai Shinbun* (*Japan Economic Journal*), 8 February 1992.

As I have repeatedly emphasised throughout this book, the average profitability of Japanese companies has been low and has continued to decline over time. However there is one area in which Japanese profitability has never declined, or at least not until very recently. That area is gross margin, or revenue minus the production cost of goods sold, which directly reflects the manufacturers' margin at the production or factory level. Why has it not deteriorated until recently? When manufacturers set the export prices for the international markets they start with direct production costs and then add a reasonable margin. Had they not done this they would be charged with overseas dumping. Therefore the only way to continue to be better and cheaper was to make the factory as lean, and efficient as possible. Factories were mostly located in rural areas where relatively cheap young or part-time workers were abundantly available. Many companies made heavy use of a large number of small subcontractors, the just-in-time production system and QC (quality control circle) activities. In addition many Japanese factories automated their operations to the maximum possible extent during the 1970s and 1980s. If you look only at their production sites, many large Japanese companies are in fact very efficient and productive even today.

In the case of US capitalism, an automated and efficient factory normally means a reduction in the workforce, leading to an efficient and profitable company. In the case of Japan, however, this has often not been the case. Because Japanese managers believe in harmony among employees, surplus workers could not and should not be laid off. Rather they have been transferred to other parts of the company, mostly to marketing, planning, coordination and general administration. Many idle or older employees have been transferred to subsidiaries and affiliated companies in the same group. As a result, sales and general administration expenses have increased. Here again Japanese capitalism has forced Japanese manufacturers to suboptimise at the cost of overall inefficiency, a necessary cost of maintaining the life-long employment commitment.

13.2.5 Major Misallocation of Resources

Another weakness of Japanese capitalism is the massive misallocation of resources. Because allocation has been based on the consensus judgment of the ruling elite rather than the strict discipline of financial performance, the system lacks a built-in mechanism to correct major misallocations of capital and other resources.

When a US company decides to invest in new plant and equipment, it typically gives serious consideration to the trade-off between the advantages of expanded scale and the possible drag on financial performance stemming from the new investment. Because the market imposes serious penalties on management if their financial performance deteriorates, there is a natural reluctance on the part of managers to undertake new investment unless the anticipated returns are sufficiently attractive to justify the risk.

In contrast, because the traditional Japanese approach attached much greater importance to the economic benefits that came from expansion in scale, new investments – even those that do not promise to be sufficiently profitable – were approved rather easily. The nature of the system also ensures the survival of most firms, especially in the external market. Consequently the Japanese system has been strongly biased towards overexpansion. Japanese companies and banks have flooded foreign markets with exports and investment to the point where it has become politically difficult for the host countries to accept any longer.

It could be said that the system has succeeded because it lacked an effective braking mechanism, and that its very success has contributed to its breakdown. External misallocation has taken the form of a huge surplus in Japan's balance of payments. In the latter half of the 1980s, internal misallocation took the form of a major bubble in stock market and real estate investment. These misallocations have rapidly undermined the consensus within and outside Japan that for a long time underpinned Japanese capitalism.

14 The Future: New Challenges and Changes

14.1 NEW CHALLENGES

Japan's traditional financial system was designed to support its economic development. The acquisition of foreign exchange through exports allowed firms to increase their investment in plant and equipment, leading to rapid growth of the economy, employment and national income levels. The system strengthened the international competitiveness of large companies – the key players in this process – and for the most part this was supported and considered desirable as long as the consensus inside and outside Japan was that Japan should prove itself an economic success under the Cold War regime. But in a way the system proved too effective, and its 'legitimacy' came to be questioned. Although the system was effective in mobilising resources to achieve certain goals at any cost, it was inefficient in that it accommodated low efficiency and low profitability. If we paraphrase the argument of Paul Klugman, Japan's capitalism was excellent at mobilising peoples' savings through its financial system, but it was not good at utilising them productively.[1] This section discusses the major forces challenging the traditional financial and management system, and the implications for the future.

14.1.1 External Imbalance

A natural consequence of Japan's 'better and cheaper' strategy has been that Japan has built up a substantial surplus in its international balance of payments. Until quite recently the

Japanese system was tolerated in part because there was a consensus among the United States and other Western nations, forged during the Cold War, that Japan should be encouraged to develop as a peaceful, economically strong nation. Reinforcing this was the openness of the international marketplace and its willingness to accommodate minor differences in national approach; great importance was attached to the notion that accepting competitive new entrants was good for the discipline of the market as well as benefiting consumers. Accordingly, in the days when Japan had a small market presence, Japanese companies were welcomed rather than shunned, and their unique management approach even came in for praise.

However, it was only a matter of time before the behaviour of Japanese companies (and of the system supporting them) came into question, especially when – one after another – US companies with a good financial performance were either driven out of business or acquired by Japanese companies whose profitability was inferior.

The Cold War is now a relic of the past. Competition among nations is rapidly shifting from military to economic dimensions, as evidenced by recent US opinion polls showing a marked rise in the view that Japan poses the 'greatest threat' to the United States.[2] It would not be surprising if this revisionist view were to take hold in other Western nations as the public reexamines Japan in the light of the new economic realities – namely that Japan's uniqueness is not due merely to a subtly difference in nuance on the same basic philosophy of capitalism and the market economy, but instead stems from a system based on completely different values and philosophies.

The fact that Japan continues to achieve a current account surplus to the scale of 100 billion dollars per annum despite the US–Japan Structural Impediment Initiative talks and the sharp revaluation of yen, clearly tells us that Japan's production capacity has surpassed its consumption capacity by that amount. Naturally the high yen has prompted Japanese manufacturers to go beyond the national boundaries to continue their operations. As the 1990s unfolded there was a massive outflow of foreign direct investment by major Japanese automobile, electrical and electronics companies which used to be the main engine of Japan's domestic growth and exports. Of course the main incentive for them to go overseas is to produce where costs are low so that they can deliver their 'better and cheaper' products not only to their traditional export markets, but to the home market, which is now the most lucrative market for many consumer goods.

This marks a major departure from the traditional behaviour of large Japanese companies, which until recently have tried to remain good citizens of Japan. In a way the large Japanese manufacturers have outgrown Japan and have joined forces with any nation for whom economic efficiency is the main criterion of decision making. If this is the case, it marks the beginning of the end of the traditional Japanese management system, which was based in Japan and operated by Japanese for the coexistence and coprosperity of the Japanese people. The implications of this are extensive.

14.1.2 The Bursting of the Bubble

It is true to say that the Japanese postwar system attached great importance to equality of outcome (in contrast with the pure free market system, which continues to emphasise equality of opportunity to participate), and that on the path to becoming an economic superpower Japan created unparalleled economic equality among its people. It is also fair to assume that the majority of the population supported the system because of this achievement.

Yet as Japan emerged as a financial powerhouse in the mid 1980s, the domestic conditions supporting the system began to crumble rapidly. Becoming a major financial power meant that there was no longer a need as a nation to absorb capital centrally and channel it into strategic areas. It heralded the arrival of an economy in which financial institutions, corporations and individual households with ample funds to invest would make their own judgements about risk and return, and manage their own financial affairs. In short the very economic success of Japan had given rise to the need for a freer and more open financial system.

It seems that nobody – not politicians, nor bureaucrats, bankers or corporate managers, let alone the general public – was prepared for such a shift. We now know the outcome: in the latter half of the 1980s vast sums were spent on unsound investments, and the immense liquidity thus created sustained huge speculative bubbles in many areas of the economy. Those who enjoyed the benefits of all this were by no means the wage earners and salaried workers who had sustained Japan's economic growth through sheer hard work. During the bubble years there was a rapid widening of the relative wealth gap between those with assets and those without.

The bubble and its demise seriously undermined the support of the Japanese people for the traditional establishment. For the first time, people grew skeptical about their elite; the legitimacy of the power and discretion exerted by the Ministry of Finance and the Bank of Japan came under scrutiny, the bureaucratic system was increasingly criticised and the banks and the banking system lost credibility among the people.

14.1.3 Financial Deregulation

The financial deregulation implemented in the 1980s, accelerated by the agreement of the Japan–US Yen–Dollar Committee in 1984, was the driving force behind several recent developments in the Japanese financial system.

The short-term effect of deregulation was to encourage the development of bubbles in the land and stock markets by encouraging performance competition throughout the entire financial services industry. Until then the industry had been strictly segmented, and tightly regulated, controlled and protected. Abundant liquidity, declining interest rates and the sudden pressure to compete for higher financial returns encouraged speculation in land and stocks on a massive scale – an easy but very risky way to create short-term returns at the expense of the long-term stability of financial institutions.

Speculation spread through the entire economy, involving financial and non-financial companies of all sizes as well as the household sector.

Another short-term effect of financial deregulation was the triggering of systematic arbitrage operations in the Japanese stock market through the introduction of stock index futures and options. In 1987 the Osaka Stock Exchange began trading stock index futures. In 1988 Osaka introduced the Nikkei index option and Tokyo introduced the TOPIX option. Chicago and Symex also began trading futures and options on Japanese stock indices. For the first time it became possible for investors to shortsell the entire stock market systematically, thus creating investors (mostly professional) who had an incentive to bet against the market and who would benefit handsomely if it declined. It is generally believed that these stock index futures and options were at least partly responsible for the major stock market adjustment that took place after 1990, marking the beginning of the end of the traditional call-optionised stock market.

In the long run, financial deregulation and the pressure on banks and other financial institutions to perform better may well have been the most important factor behind the change from the traditional relationship-based system to one based more on arm's-length relations among companies and between companies and financial institutions. Financial institutions seeking higher returns for depositors and investors will find it very difficult to continue to support the low-return strategy of their traditional corporate partners. This means that the entire set of traditional relationships will have to be reviewed in the new light of financial returns, including a thorough reassessment of relationship stock investment and cross-holding arrangements.

14.1.4 Globalisation

Globalisation has come increasingly to dominate the economic and business environment in the 1990s. It is an immense force, not only in absorbing inferior systems into a superior one (as symbolised by the collapse of the former Soviet-led centrally planned economies and the fall of the Berlin Wall), but also in compelling successful but unique systems to conform to the norms of a more widely accepted and more universal system. Japan obviously faces this latter challenge.

The guiding principles in creating a global system are the development of common standards for all important matters and the reciprocal acceptance of local rules for more technical matters. The former includes the harmonisation, at least among industrialised nations, of rules dealing with fair competition, intellectual property rights, environmental issues, financial reporting and disclosure, and bank regulations.

In the context of the discussion in this chapter, the harmonisation of fair trade laws has the potential to affect the Japanese system significantly. The entire concept of the traditional Japanese *keiretsu* and business groups was a key issue at the structural impediment Initiative talks.[3] More specifically, if the customary long-term, interlocking relationships between the main banks and their corporate clients do indeed involve preferential and reciprocal business dealings, as is often claimed, their legitimacy will increasingly come under scrutiny in the light of global fair competition.

The new Bank for International Settlements (BIS) rule on bank equity capital can also be expected to have a substantial impact on Japan's financial system. The BIS rule requires all international banks to maintain an equity capital cushion of at least 8 per cent of risk-weighted business loans and investments. Loans and investments to all private companies are classified under the same risk category, even if the borrower is a well-established, large company with a longstanding relationship with the bank. In other words the BIS rule means that the banks' relationships with private companies must be at arm's-length. If they are to abide by the rule, the large banks will have to reassess their entire set of traditional relationship in order to achieve higher returns on assets. This will make it very difficult for them to provide preferential terms of lending to or investment in selected corporate customers.

14.1.5 Japan's Aging Society

At about the same time as it became an economic and financial superpower, Japan also became one of the world's lowest-growth nations in terms of labour supply. According to recent official demographic statistics, the average Japanese woman has 1.53 children (sometimes referred to as the '1.53 shock'). The Japanese labour force will begin to decline in 2001 and the population will peak in about 2006. The aging of society will also accelerate. The proportion of the population aged 65 years and over will exceed 20 per cent by 2010 and will approach 30 per cent by 2020.[4]

Together with the longer than average life expectancy, these demographic trends are rapidly turning Japan into a 'pension' state, where life after retirement is a major concern for many citizens. With the stock of household financial assets exceeding 1000 trillion yen, the efficient management of financial assets in general, and of corporate and government pensions in particular, is becoming a very important issue.

These emerging needs of the Japanese people may well encourage large companies and financial institutions to manage much more efficiently the capital entrusted to them.

14.1.6 Restructuring the Entire Economic System

The traditional financial and management system, with its heavy emphasis on economic growth, was supported by a general consensus that, above all, Japan needed fully to employ its labour force, the country's most abundant and probably most precious economic resource. It was this consensus that legitimised the strategic allocation of economic resources in general, and of capital in particular. The goals of the system have largely been achieved, creating new demands on Japanese companies from domestic and international stakeholders. Today, an increase in the size of the economic pie, with growth in investments, production and exports and the creation of more jobs, is no longer as desirable. Rather, Japan now needs a system that will make more efficient use of scarce resources while at the same time meeting the new and diversified demands of its people, who are increasingly seeking a better-quality life.

A free market approach guided by the 'invisible hand' seems more compatible with these new economic goals than the traditional system of allocating resources based on the consensus judgement of the elite and on long-term, interlocking relationships.

In the open market approach, the primary role of large companies and financial institutions is, as professional management entities, to make the best possible use of scarce economic resources. Financial institutions will be expected to perform as professional managers with fiduciary responsibility for managing the financial assets of their clients. In short, both firms and financial institutions will be increasingly judged by their financial efficiency.

14.2 SOME EVIDENCE OF CHANGE

It is uncertain how long it will take for these early signs of change to mature. There will, of course, be a transition period in which forces for and against change may clash. But the fundamental shift from strategic allocation to a more open market system seems inevitable. The following provides some evidence that such a change is in train.

14.2.1 Disappearance of the Cost-of-Capital Advantage

Mainly because of the major stock market decline since 1990, Japan's cost-of-capital advantage has largely disappeared. The Economic Planning Agency estimated that the average cost of capital for Japan had risen to approximately the same level as in the United States by 1991.[5] Malkiel agrees that by early 1992 the average cost of capital in the United States, Japan and Germany had converged to similar levels.[6] If this is the case, Japanese companies will be unable to expand any further on the basis of low-cost capital, marking the end of the low-return strategy. Unless they can achieve higher profitability, they will find it increasingly difficult to attract capital for growth.

14.2.2 The Breakdown of Cross-Ownership Arrangements

Partly because of the BIS rule and partly because of the current severe recession, both banks and companies are beginning to liquidate part of their relationship equity investments in order to improve accounting profits and/or cash flows. It seems that the cost of maintaining the cross-ownership arrangement is now becoming too high and the benefits are diminishing.

14.2.3 The Declining Role of the Main Banks as Delegated Monitors

Traditionally, it was assumed that the main banks would always remain committed, stable shareholders, and because of this outside investors regarded them as delegated monitors of the stock market. Although banks occasionally sold part of their relationship portfolios in order to realise capital gains for reporting and other purposes, they almost always simultaneously bought back the same number of stocks in the same companies at essentially the same prices, through so-called cross-transactions.

The assumption of stable ownership on a 'net' basis was the primary rationale for the banks to count 45 per cent of the unrealised capital gains on their equity investments as second-tier equity capital under the BIS rule. However, as the need grew to write off a large number of the bad or non-performing debts that materialised after 1991, banks began to realise capital gains on their relationship equity portfolios on a massive scale. While a large part of these sales was matched by simultaneous repurchases, it was widely reported in the financial media that some banks had either sold some stocks outright, were trying to obtain consent from companies to sell outright or were shortselling stocks to realise capital gains. Indeed the massive sale of stocks by the major banks caused so much concern in the summer of 1992 that the Ministry of Finance, as part of its widely publicised price-keeping operations, strongly requested that banks refrain from the outright sale of stocks. The role of the main banks as delegated monitors of the stock market also seems to be in decline.

14.2.4 Emphasis on Corporate Profitability

My paper in Japanese, which won the Tokyo Marine Kagami Memorial Foundation prize in 1991, triggered a discussion in policy circles concerning the low-profitability orientation of the Japanese management system.[7] In February 1992 Akio Morita, chairman of the Sony Corporation, contributed a controversial article to the monthly journal, *Bungeishunju*.[8] In it he argued that the traditional Japanese approach of selling high-quality products at low prices might be at the heart of the so-called 'Japan problem' as perceived by the West.

It is now widely recognised that the profitability of Japanese companies needs to be improved. Several major companies have announced that they will raise the hurdle or cut-off rates for their new investment decisions. Some have decided to shut down unprofitable operations in North America and elsewhere. Others are emphasising improvements in profitability even at the risk of reducing the total size of their businesses. To some extent these changes have been made in response to the current severe recession. But they also reflect a fundamental shift in the priorities of large Japanese companies, from growth in size to efficiency of capital utilisation and profitability.

For investors, too, profitability measures – return on equity, dividend payout ratios and so on – are becoming the main criteria for evaluating stocks. This change may well signal the beginning of an investment approach based on the fundamental value of companies.

14.3 IMPLICATIONS FOR THE STRATEGIES OF JAPANESE COMPANIES

How will these new challenges and changes affect the strategies of Japanese companies? Should they abandon their traditional 'better and cheaper' strategy or should they maintain it in a different form? Figure 14.1 provides us with a starting point.

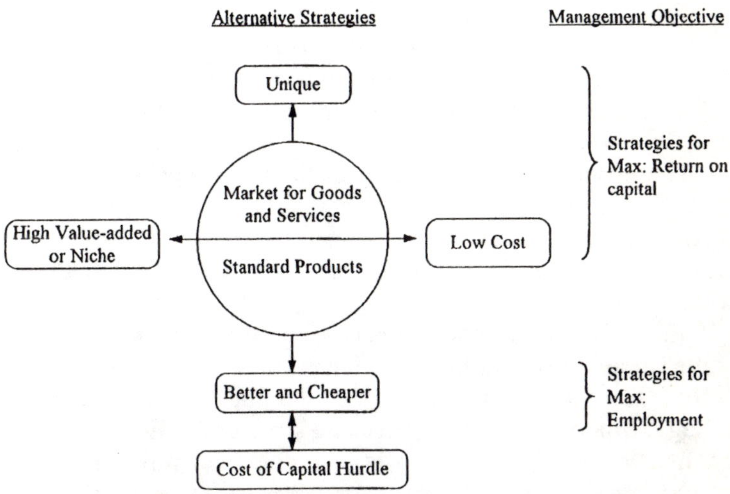

FIGURE 14.1 Strategic options for value creation

When the objective of the management is to provide maximum return on equity (ROE) it can choose between three strategies, or some combination of all three: (1) a low-cost strategy, (2) a niche strategy or (3) a unique strategy. Take a standard four-door sedan car as an example.

A low-cost approach aims at cheaper cars with essentially the same function as the standard product in the market. Since the objective is to maximise ROE, the management cannot just reduce the price. They really have to think hard about lowering their costs so that the cars can be sold cheaply but still achieve a reasonable ROE. In order to do this they introduce economies of scale, automation and a lean production system, or they go offshore to take advantage of cheap labour and so on. Companies that choose this course tend to have large-scale operations.

A niche approach cultivates a market where the customers are willing to pay extra if the product delivers some unique value to them. Specialising in expensive sports cars is one example of this. Getting it right may bring in a comfortable ROE, but the size of the market is usually limited and the companies that choose this course tend to remain small.

A unique strategy aims at creating something that does not yet exist and no one can be sure that it is commercially feasible. Therefore this is the riskiest of the three, but if it is done right it may bring the greatest returns. Developing a car that runs on solar energy is one example. In reality most large car manufacturers use some combination of all three strategies.

If the objective is not to maximise ROE but to maximise employment, production, exports or some other size-related factor, there is one more choice: the 'better and cheaper' strategy. Since in this case there is a structural advantage of a low hurdle rate, a car that costs as much as or more than the standard product to produce can be sold at a lower price but in greater numbers. Since the open market welcomes any product that is better and/or cheaper, the company is certain to survive and grow in size.

However if Japanese companies start to lose their structural advantage of low-cost capital, then the traditional choice of 'better and cheaper' will become harder to continue. Consequently many will have to turn to the first three strategic options in line with the practices of Anglo-American management. Nonetheless many will continue to pursue the 'better and cheaper' approach in the global context. Figure 14.2 illustrates this possibility. Many have already started to go global, and there has been heavy investment in South-East Asia and China in recent years.

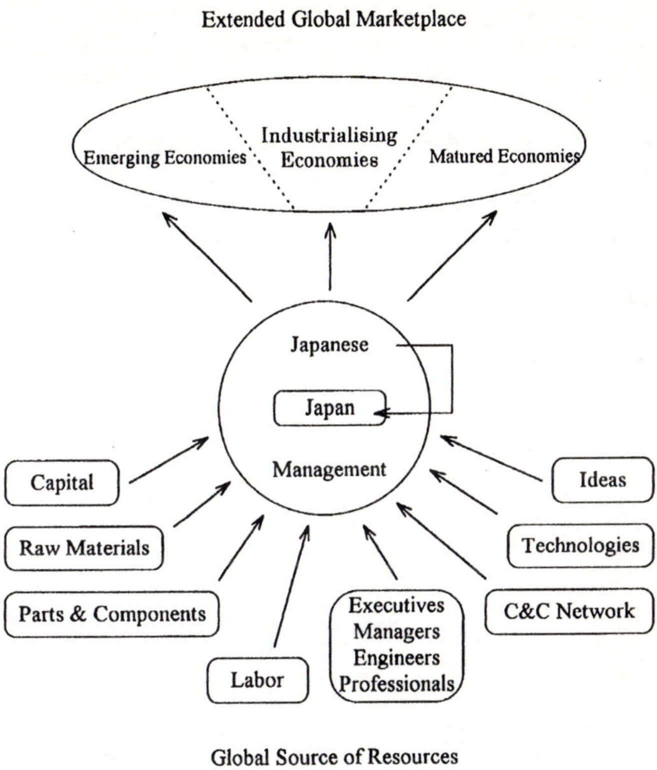

FIGURE 14.2 New paradigm of Japanese management

The international market expanded phenomenally after the collapse of the Berlin Wall in 1989. Russia, the Eastern European nations and mainland China have all joined the broadly defined market economy and a vast new market for labour, raw materials, industrial goods and capital has opened up for everyone. Standard electronic components are readily available in many parts of the world, including North-East and South-East Asia and North America. The rapid development in telecommunications has created an information age in which traditional national borders mean little for the management of companies. Likewise the movement of people across national borders has accelerated, so unskilled labour and professional skills are also readily available in many parts of the world.

In this extended global marketplace, it is quite possible and natural that some large Japanese companies will maintain their traditional value-creation approach of 'better and cheaper'. Only this time it will be undertaken in the global context, not by the Japanese, for the Japanese nor based on the island of Japan.

Notes and References

1 Economic Systems and Resource Allocation

1. H. Iwaki, 'Coordination of Competition, Policies for Fair Global Competition', *NRI Quarterly*, vol. 1 no. 2 (Nomura Research Institute, 1992), pp. 22–39.
2. C. Johnson, *MITI and the Japanese Miracle* (Tokyo: Charles E. Tuttle, 1986) p. 10.

2 Economic Value Creation by Investor-Owned Companies

1. T. K. McCraw (ed.), *America versus Japan* (Boston: Harvard Business School Press, 1986), p. 26.

4 Two Approaches to Stock Valuation

1. J. M. Keynes, *General Theory of Employment, Interest and Money* (London: Macmillan, 1936), chapter 12.
2. B. Graham, D. L. Dodd, S. Cottle and C. Tatham, *Security Analysis*, 4th edn (New York: McGraw-Hill, 1962).
3. Extract from S. Cottle, unpublished lecture notes for Nomura Research Institute (Tokyo: Nomura Research Institute, 1972).
4. E. F. Fama, 'Efficient Capital Markets: A Review of Theory and Empirical Work', *Journal of Finance*, vol. 25, no. 5 (May 1970), pp. 383–417.
5. More and more researchers are discovering that the US stock market is not that efficient. Stock market phenomena that contradict the efficient market hypothesis are called market anomalies. For a discussion of market anomalies, see, for example, B. I. Jacobs and K. N. Levy, 'Disentangling Equity Return Regularities: New Insights and Investment Opportunities', *Financial Analysts Journal*, May – June 1988.
6. W. F. Sharpe and G. J. Alexander, *Investments*, 4th edn (New Jersey: Prentice-Hall, 1990), pp. 77–80.

7. A. D. Chandler, 'The Enduring Logic of Industrial Success', *Harvard Business Review*, vol. 68, no. 2 (1990), pp. 130–40.

5 Japanese Economic and Financial Systems

1. C. Johnson, *MITI and the Japanese Miracle* (Tokyo: Charles E. Tuttle, 1986), p. 10.
2. For further discussions of the unique features of the Japanese economic system, see C. Johnson, *MITI and the Japanese Miracle*, (Tokyo: Charles E. Tuttle, 1986); Y. Noguchi, *1940 Nen Taisei (1940 Regime)*, (Tokyo: Toyo Keizai, 1995); D. I. Okimoto, *Between MITI and the Market* Stanfrod, CA: Stanford University Press, 1989).
3. Y. Suzuki (ed.), *The Japanese Financial System* (Oxford: Oxford University Press, 1987), p. 23.
4. Ibid, p. 22.
5. K. E. Calder, *Strategic Capitalism* (Princeton, NJ: Princeton University Press, 1993).
6. Economic Planning Agency, *Heisei 4 Nendo Keizai Hakusho* (*1992 Economic White Paper*) (Tokyo, 1993), p. 249.

6 The Unique Features of the Japanese Stock and Share Ownership Structure

1. Ministry of Trade and Industry (ed.) *Comparison of the Behaviour of Japanese and US Firms* (Tokyo: MITI, 1989), pp. 100–1 (in Japanese)
2. Fair Trade Commission, *Report on the Actual Condition of the Six Major Corporate Groups* (Tokyo, 1994), pp. 22–37.
3. I. Nakatani, 'The Economic Role of Financial Corporate Grouping', in M. Aoki (ed.), *The Economic Analysis of the Japanese Firm* (Amsterdam: North-Holland, 1984), pp. 227–58.
4. Fair Trade Commission, op. cit., pp. 88–107.
5. It is interesting to note that the concept of 'relationship investing' has been discussed in the United States recently. See, for example, M. E. Porter, 'Capital Disadvantage: America's Failing Capital Investment System', *Harvard Business Review*, vol. 70, no. 5 (1992) pp. 65–82; 'Relationship Investing', *Business Week*, 15 March 1993, pp. 38–45.

9 Factors Underpinning the Call-Optionalisation of the Stock Market

1. F. Takahashi, 'Fundamental Information and Stock Price Formation in Japan', *Security Analysts Journal*, vol. 30, no. 3 (May 1991), pp. 1–13, (in Japanese).

2. F. Takahashi, 'Information' on Corporate Fundamental and Stock Prices in the US and Japan, unpublished paper presented at the Osaka University Conference on Corporate Financial Policy and International Competition, January 1992, Osaka, Japan.
3. For more details of the role of main banks, see P. Sheard, 'Interlocking Shareholding and Corporate Governance', in M. Aoki and R. Dore (eds), *The Japanese Firms: The Sources of Competitive Strength* (Oxford: Clarendon Press 1994), pp. 310–49.

10 Corporate Profitability and International Competition

1. J. C. Abegglen and G. Stalk, Jr., *Kaisha–The Japanese Corporation* (Tokyo: Charles E. Tuttle, 1985), p. 70.

11 International Comparison of the Cost of Capital

1. R. N. McCauley and S. A. Zimer, International Comparison of the Cost of Capital, *Shoken Analysts Journal (Security Analysts Journal)* vol. 30, no. 3 (1992), pp. 12–28.
2. B. G. Malkiel, 'The Concept and International Comparison of the Cost of Capital' *Shoken analysts Journal* (*Security Analysts Journal*), vol. 30, no. 3 (1992), pp. 29–36.
3. J. M. Poterba, 'Comparing the Cost of Capital in the United States and Japan: A Survey of Methods, *Federal Reserve Bank of New York Quarterly Reveiew*, vol. 16, no. 4 (1991).
4. J. A. Frankel, 'Japanese Finance in the 1980s: A Survey', in P. Krugman (ed.), *Trade with Japan: Has the Door Opened Wider*? (New York: Wiley, 1991), pp. 22–37.
5. See, for example, *The Banker*, July 1987, pp. 69–179.
6. R. N. McCauley and S. A. Zimmer, 'Bank Cost of Capital and International Competition', *Federal Reserve Bank of New York Quarterly Review*, vol. 16, no. 4 (1991), pp. 33–59.
7. P. Sheard, op. cit.
8. Fair Trade Commission, op. cit.

12 Japan's National Value-Creation System

1. H. Itami, *Jinpon-shugi Kigyou* (*Peopleism Company*) (Tokyo: Chikuma Shobo, 1987)

13 The Merits and Demerits of Japanese Capitalism

1. World Bank, *The East Asian Miracle* (Oxford: Oxford University Press, 1993).
2. Ibid., p. 9.

14 The Future: New Challenges and Changes

1. P. Krugman, 'The Myth of Asia's Miracle', *Foreign Affairs*, vol. 73, no. 6 (1994), pp. 62–78.
2. Yomiuri Shinbun, 22 July 1992.
3. Final report, *US–Japan* Structural Impediment *Initiatives*, (1990), Tokyo: Japanese ministry of Foreign affairs.
4. Ministry of Welfare, *1990 Nendo Jinko Dotai Tokei* (*1990 Demographic Statistics Year Book*) (Tokyo, 1991).
5. Economic Planning Agency, op. cit., p. 252.
6. B. G. Malkiel, 'The Concept of Cost of Capital', *Security Analysts Journal*, vol. 30, no. 3 (March 1992), pp. 29–36.
7. M. Ide, 'Nihon Keizai wa Ishitsuka' (Is Japan's Economy Unique?) (Tokyo: Tokyo Marine Kagami Memorial Foundation, 1991.
8. A. Morita, 'Nihongata Keiei ga Abunai' (Japanese Style Management is in Danger), *Bungei Shunju*, vol. 70, no. 2 (1992), pp. 94–103.

Index

agency costs 75
arbitrage operations 177
arbitrage pricing theory (APT) 42
automobile companies 163

balance of payments 172, 173–5
Bank for International Settlements (BIS) 77, 101, 103, 119, 178, 181
banks
  commercial 76–7
  as delegated monitors 117–19, 181–2
  problems for 102, 103
  regulated system 77
  relationship with companies 72
  role 61–2
  unrealised capital gain 94–5
  see also relationship investment
Berlin Wall 186
better and cheaper strategy 20–1, 25, 78, 125–8, 163, 167, 184–5, 186
bonds 97
Bretton Woods system 13, 127, 153

Calder, K. E. 62
capital
  accumulation 164
  debt 21, 27, 29–30
  diverse sources of 71–2
  empirical findings 142–8
  equity 21, 25, 27, 29–30
  return on 21–2
capital asset pricing model (CAPM) 42, 50
capital cost
  concept 141–2
  increasing 180–1
capital cost (*cont.*)
  low 62, 125–6, 135, 137
capitalist economy 4
  see also US capitalism
cash flow
  expected 44
  forecasts 46
  'slicing' 34–7
  as source of value 27–30, 33
centrally planned economies 59
Chandler, A. 47
Cold War 174
companies
  as black boxes 45–6
  efficient 169–71
  evaluation rules 23–6, 30–4, 49
  financial ratios 63–7
  financing policy 63–8
  fundamentals 40
  as going concerns 30–4
  and governments 17–18
  growth 78–80, 137–40, 145
  net income 112
  ownership and management 46–7, 76
  performance 22, 128–32
  relationship with shareholders 51–2
  strategies 183–6
  strategically important 61–2
  value creation 17–26, 151–4
competition
  banking 147
  and efficiency prices 50–1
  international 127, 174
  and profitability 133–7
  strategies 20–1
constant growth rate model 34
Cottle, S. 40
cross-holding 71, 73, 81, 99, 181

cross-transactions 119
debt cost 142, 145
debt to equity ratio 66
deregulation 57, 176–7
developmental capitalist states 55
dividends 98
  expected 33–4, 87–8, 90
  fixed 87–9
  per share (DPS) 80
dollars 166

earnings before interest and tax (EBIT) 133
earnings per share (EPS) 80
East Asia 159–60, 166
economic growth
  goal of 151
  international comparisons 159–64
  and profitability 139
  stable 162–3
efficiency
  defined 44
  low 168–71
  prices 44–52, 75
efficient market hypothesis 42–3
employment goal 153, 166, 171, 184
equality 9, 59, 159, 160
equilibrium theory 42
equity 175
  at par value 87, 94, 99
  capital 21, 25, 27, 29–30, 62
  cost 142, 143, 145, 147–8
  market price 85, 97–102
  new 82–6, 87, 94, 97–102
  preemptive subscription right 91–2
  return on (ROE) 23–4, 66, 78–9, 108, 139, 142, 158
  rule 77, 101, 103, 119, 178, 181
  see also securities; shares; stocks
exchange rate 127

face-to-face negotiations 59, 68, 70
Fama 41
financial institutions 60
financial system 56–7
  indirect 60–2
  open 176
foreign exchange 61
Frankel, J. A. 145

globalisation 57, 177–8, 186
Graham, B. 40

hard currency 127, 154, 155–6
human resources 164

IMF 99
incentives 9
information 42, 75, 118
interest rates 125, 141–2
internal rate of return (IRR) 29
investment
  new projects 139
  performance indicators 109–10
  see also relationship investment
investors
  conflicting interests 36–7
  institutional 47–9, 51
  small 92
Itami, H. 153

Japan
  in central marketplace 14–15
  national strategy 154
  system limitations 164–72
Johnson, C. 55

keiretsu 61–2, 178
Keynes, J. M. 40
Klugman, P. 173

local optimisation 166–7

McCauley, R. N. 142, 146, 148
Malkiel, B. G. 142, 145, 180

management
  objectives 184
  and ownership 46–7, 76
  system of 156–8
managers 22, 23
market
  efficient 45
  free 180
  international 155, 166, 177–8, 186
  open 3, 10–12, 155, 166
  psychology of 39–40
Ministry of International Trade and Industry (MITI) 56, 69, 156
modern portfolio theory (MPT) 41–3, 49–50
Morita, A. 182

neoclassical economics 11–12, 166
networks 56
Nikkei index 177

openness index 10

pension funds 48–9
'peopleism' 153
population, aging 179
post-war reconstruction 13
Poterba, J. M. 145
price-keeping operations (PKOs) 108
price–earnings ratio (PER) 34, 78–9, 82, 85, 127, 137
product differentiation 18, 20
productivity 168–9
profit
  indicators 110–12
  maximisation 167
profitability 63
  and company growth 137–40, 145
  and competition 133–7
  and economic growth 139
  low 133–7, 158, 171
  need for improvement 182
  US/Japan comparison 128–32
protectionism 167–8

relationship investment 99, 102
  characteristics of 73–7
  and liability management 76–8
  purpose of 81
  see also banks
resource allocation
  methods of 3–7
  misallocation 172
  strategic 55–9, 125
restructuring 179–80
risk 49–50, 120
  aversion 25
  default 77
  hedging system 107–8
  interest rate 76–7
  investment 103
  premium 29
  taking 24–5
Roos, D. 163

sales 112
Samuelson, P. A. 41
securities 36
  see also equity; shares; stocks
shares
  free distribution 82, 95, 102
  motives of owners 73, 75
  ownership structure 69–73
  see also equity; securities; stocks
Sharpe, W. 41, 44–5
socialist centrally planned economy 3, 8–9
states
  and companies 17–18
  control by 56
  regulatory 11
stock market
  call-optionised 104, 107
  company valuation 23–4
  crash 101, 120

stock market (*cont.*)
  Osaka 177
  role of 27
  unique Japanese features 78–80, 120–1
  US 44, 48, 113, 115
stock prices 46, 82
  average 93–4
  behaviour of 85, 92–3, 98–9
  efficient 44–52, 75
  rising 108
  US and Japan 104–6
stock valuation 87–95, 103–6
  'beauty contest' 40, 108–16
  empirical evidence 109–16
  technical and fundamental analysis 39–41
stocks
  call option 115, 117–19
  common 81–2, 103, 116
  illiquid 81
  portfolios 112–16
  see also equity; securities; shares
Structural Impediment Initiative (SII) 4, 174, 178
submarkets 57–8

technology 156, 158
Tobin, J. 41
TOPIX 177
trade
  fair 178
  multilateral 153–4
trust 37

United States
  antitrust laws 13, 57
  as central marketplace 12–15
  companies and governments 17
  Employee Retirement Income Security Act 49
  historical development 12–13
  institutional investors 51
  stock market 44, 48, 113, 115
  'wash sale' 119
  in world system 3
  see also Structural Impediment Initiative (SII)
US capitalism 11, 78, 118, 151, 171
  as international public good 13–14
  risk-taking 25
  see also capitalist economy

World Bank 159

zero-sum game 167
Zimmer, S. A. 142, 146, 148